Spy of the Century

A man may commit a disloyal or base act, even the worst, even murder, and yet remain blameless. The act does not constitute the whole truth, it is always and only a consequence. (Sándor Márai, Embers)

Spy of the Century

*Alfred Redl and the Betrayal
of Austria-Hungary*

John Sadler
and Silvie Fisch

Pen & Sword
MILITARY

First published in Great Britain in 2016 by
PEN AND SWORD HISTORY
an imprint of
Pen and Sword Books Ltd
47 Church Street
Barnsley
South Yorkshire S70 2AS

ISBN 978 1 47384 870 2

Printed and bound in England
by CPI Group (UK) Ltd, Croydon, CR0 4YY

Typeset in Times New Roman by
CHIC GRAPHICS

Pen & Sword Books Ltd incorporates the imprints of Pen & Sword
Archaeology, Atlas, Aviation, Battleground, Discovery,
Family History, History, Maritime, Military, Naval, Politics, Railways,
Select, Social History, Transport, True Crime, Claymore Press,
Frontline Books, Leo Cooper, Praetorian Press, Remember When,
Seaforth Publishing and Wharncliffe.

For a complete list of Pen and Sword titles please contact
Pen and Sword Books Limited
47 Church Street, Barnsley, South Yorkshire, S70 2AS, England
E-mail: enquiries@pen-and-sword.co.uk
Website: www.pen-and-sword.co.uk

Contents

List of Illustrations

The Imperial Hofburg Palace in Vienna (Michaeler Wing), between 1890 and 1900
Habsburg Castle, *Topographia Helvetiae* (Matthäus Merian, 1642)
Lemberg around 1900
Emperor Franz Joseph I, c.1880
Political cartoon depicting the Afghan Emir Sher Ali with his 'friends' the Russian Bear and British Lion. Text: 'Save me from my friends.' Sir John Tenniel, *Punch Magazine*, 30 November 1878
Alois Lexa von Aehrenthal
Guy Percy Wyndham and his brother George
K.u.k. Infantry, Galicia, 1898
Galician Infantry Regiment, Lemberg, 1884: Alfred Redl is listed under 'Cadets'
Threat of war in the Balkans
The seal of the Evidenzbureau
The blood-stained uniform of Archduke Franz Ferdinand of Austria
Nicholas II, Emperor of Russia, c.1909
Railway Map Austria Hungary 1911 (*Encyclopaedia Britannica*)
Cover of the *Petit Journal*, 20 January 1895 (illustration by Lionel Royer and Fortuné Méaulle)
Austrian War Ministry Building, Am Hof (demolished in 1913)
Former Imperial and Royal Ministry of War
Military Directory from 1905, Alfred Redl is now listed as 'general staff/Evidenzbureau'
Roth, Joseph, *Radetzkymarsch*, 1st edn, Berlin, 1932 (photo H-P. Haack)
Kaiser Wilhelm II and Philipp, Prince of Eulenburg, 1890
Franz Conrad von Hoetzendorf in 1915
Oscar Wilde's trial, *Police News*, 4 May 1895

Egon Erwin Kisch, GDR stamp 1985

'Photo-Notebook' camera by Rudolph Krügener, 1888 (Musée des Arts et Métiers)

Alfred Redl and Baron von Giesl in an open carriage in Prague (© ÖNB)

Marianna (May) Török de Szendrö

A 20-crown banknote of the Dual Monarchy

Vienna Central Cemetery (Find A Grave). Nothing survives of Alfred Redl. His remains are buried under the wooden boards (which were used during the digging of a recent grave).

Klaus Maria Brandauer as Colonel Redl in Istvén Szabó's 1985 film

A Patriot for Me at the Scala Theatre, Vienna, 2015 (photo Bettina Frenzel)

Hotel Klomser, Vienna, c.1910 (© ÖNB)

Preface

If you involve yourself in history and get excited by real spy stories, it's quite likely that you have come across the man who has been nicknamed 'spy of the century'. When we first heard of Alfred Redl, we were fascinated by the alleged scale of his betrayal and its consequences. But the deeper we looked into his case, the more doubts arose: was he really the evil, reckless man who was responsible for the deaths of 'tens of thousands of men' in the First World War? It soon became clear that fact and fiction had become inextricably entangled. The history of the scandal and attempts to sweep the dirt under the carpet turned out to be even more fascinating than that of the betrayal itself. A story of human tragedy emerged, of a man who was forced to hide his homosexuality, and attempted to use his position and wealth to satisfy his needs.

This book could not have been written without outstanding research by two Austrian historians, Verena Moritz and Hannes Leidinger. Right after Redl's death some of the compromising documents and photographs were burnt. In tandem with the collapse of the Habsburg monarchy, many archive materials were destroyed in 1918 to avoid them falling into enemy hands. Many more got lost during the Second World War. But worst of all, what had been left in the Austrian State Archives was misplaced, most probably deliberately, to safeguard the army's reputation. Many years later, in 1994, the German historian Guenther Kronenbitter rediscovered the 'lost' files in the Vienna archives. Also in the 1990s, relevant material in Moscow became accessible.

Moritz and Leidinger, who also used archive materials from the UK, France and Italy, set out to fill in the gaps and to separate true from false. They published their research in 2012 in Austria (*Oberst Redl: Der Spionagefall, der Skandal, die Fakten*). Together with the wealth of digital resources available from the Austrian State Archives, their findings provided the ideal starting point for our own project. Despite the many films, plays and novels and despite the importance of the scandal in the run-up to the First World War, the Redl case will never be 100 per cent demystified. Up to now Alfred Redl has not had a factual English biography. Yet, as Moritz and Leidinger put it: 'If you're looking for definitive truth, you'd better stop reading now.'

Quotations at the start of some of the chapters are taken from a remarkable polemic *Is Austria Doomed* by Countess Zanardi Landi and published by Hodder & Stoughton in 1916, at the height of the Great War. Her real name was Caroline Kaiser-Kuhnott and she claimed to be the daughter of Empress Elizabeth.

As ever, the authors remain responsible for any and all errors or omissions and whilst every effort has been made to trace copyright holders and to give credits accordingly, the authors would always be grateful to hear from anyone who detects any deficiencies and will make due amends.

Silvie Fisch and John Sadler
Newcastle upon Tyne, December 2015

Chapter 1

Prelude

The enormous weight of the trunks used by some travellers not infrequently inflicts serious injury on the hotel and railway porters who have to handle them. Travellers are therefore urged to place their heavy articles in the smaller packages and thus minimize the evil as far as possible. (Baedeker, *Austria-Hungary*, 1911)

It was a chilly day for the season in Vienna, rather windy, and the occasional rain shower made things worse. Colonel Redl had travelled all the way from Prague and went straight to his room at Hotel Klomser, a striking building in the old town, part of a larger complex that had been known as the Palais Batthyány-Strattmann for almost two centuries. Why the hotel? Redl had his own flat in Vienna. Was its location not central enough? Did he prefer to remain less visible?

Vienna, the ancient capital of the Austrian Empire and residence of the Emperor, had become the capital of the Cisleithanian half of the Austrian-Hungarian Monarchy. It was the seat of the government of the grand-duchy of Lower Austria, residence of a Roman Catholic prince-archbishop, and headquarters of the 2nd Corps of the Austro-Hungarian army. Vienna covered an area almost as big as London. More than 2 million people lived here before the start of the First World War, making Vienna the fourth in size among the capitals of Europe.

The mighty Danube still flows through the city today and meets the waters of the Wien. But Redl's Vienna was a very different city then – although dominated by reactionary, conservative structures it was also an Eldorado of the arts and a capital of science, linked to names such as Egon Schiele, Oskar Kokoschka, Gustav Mahler, Arnold Schoenberg, Joseph Roth and Stefan Zweig, who wrote:

> It was an ordered world with definite classes and calm transitions, a world without haste. The rhythm of the new speed had not yet carried over from the machines, the automobile, the telephone, the radio, and the aeroplane, to mankind; time and age had another measure.[1]

On this particular day, 24 May 1913, Alfred Redl had no eyes for Vienna's beauty. Just a few hours later, in the early hours of 25 May, the former head of the counter-intelligence branch of the Intelligence Bureau of Austria-Hungary was found dead in his hotel room. He had shot himself through the mouth. The projectile was found stuck in his skull.

Why had this successful and highly regarded man decided to end his own life? His career had flourished. Only the year before, he had left his post in Vienna to become chief of staff of the 8th Army Corps in Prague. He had a bright future ahead of him, and was even regarded as a potential candidate for the post of war minister.

News about his suicide hit the local press the next day. The gun had slipped out of his hands; his whole face had been covered in blood (*Wiener Neueste Nachrichten*, 26 May 1913). They all agreed: he had been 'mentally disturbed'. This was in fact the commonly accepted explanation for suicide, with a long tradition. In pre-modern society someone who committed suicide of free will had no right to a Christian burial.

In Redl's case the reasons for his mental health problems seemed obvious. A man of duty who had dedicated his life to the army, he had worked much too hard which had led to what we nowadays call 'burnout'. *Wiener Neueste Nachrichten* called him 'one of our most driven and efficient officers of the General staff' and claimed that he had recently suffered from sleepless nights.

But while most journalists tried to outdo each other with their praise for the deceased's outstanding honesty, the first rumours started to spread. 3,000 Austrian kronen had allegedly been found in his hotel room. The *Neueste Wiener Tagblatt* announced that they had already started to investigate these claims. This was published on 26 May, just one day after the suicide. Nevertheless, a young journalist in Prague would later claim that it had been his article in the German-language newspaper *Bohemia* that had first raised doubts about this soldier's clean slate.

Egon Erwin Kisch had been born in Prague, the 'marketplace full of sensations' in 1885 and later earned a reputation as the 'raging reporter'. In his early days he had already become acquainted with 'fanatics for liberty, anti-authoritarians, egalitarians, full of hatred against cowards and strivers and militarism ... , they gave me a lot of their precious hatred for the privileged society, something I am honestly grateful for'.[2]

He started off as a local reporter, first for the *Prager Tagblatt*, then for the *Bohemia*. The *Bohemia* was a conservative paper, pro-government and anti-Czech. Kisch was only 21 years old when he got offered a job. He soon focused on the lower classes, on their everyday lives dominated by poverty, and on criminal affairs. Here, in the poorest parts of the city, in the pubs and brothels, he developed his famous style of investigative journalism. His articles got published in the paper's Saturday supplement, and they were so successful that he later published them in his book 'Adventures in Prague'.

Unfortunately for our case, Kisch wasn't always too particular about the truth. As Viera Glosíková from Charles University in Prague, puts it:

Kisch always knew that information alone is not enough. He realized he had to grab the readers' attention and amuse them. He applied literary means, lyrical touches, dialogues, descriptions, and a lot of tension. He would follow a story and only disclose its essence at the very end.[3]

Over the years Kisch published four different versions of his Redl story, and his descriptions of the course of events was mostly accepted as definitive.

Kisch claimed in several of his books that he had been the first to argue that Redl had been entangled in the world of espionage, in bold print on top of page 1 of the *Bohemia*. As a matter of fact, it was page 2 of the evening edition on 27 May, and on the same day *Die Zeit* in Vienna also mentioned a possible connection. This was a crucial turn, as *Die Zeit* was a paper read in and obtaining information from officers' circles, certainly not an anti-monarchist organ.

> Rumours are circulating in Vienna that Colonel of the General staff Redl committed the suicide we reported yesterday because he was entangled in an affair of espionage. The Officers he kept company with shortly before his death confronted him with the incriminating evidence, Colonel Redl preferred to avoid further investigations through death within a given time frame.[4]

Nevertheless, Kisch's approach was one of a kind and still entertains today, as he brought out the news in the form of a denial, to avoid the confiscation of the article:

> There was one difficulty that seemed insurmountable. How could one intimate that an Austrian chief of staff was in the pay of a foreign nation? How could one print such news in an Austrian paper without immediate confiscation? only by a surprise play. (…) We would risk the suppression of the evening edition by bringing out the news in the form of a denial.
>
> Thus, in bold and on the most prominent part of the first page, we wrote: 'We have been asked by higher authority to deny the rumours that have arisen especially in military circles, that the Chief of the General staff of the Prague Army Corps, Colonel Alfred Redl, who committed suicide the day before yesterday in Vienna, had been a spy in the service of Russia and had betrayed the military secrets of his country.' (…) Such denials are well understood by the reader. The effect is just the

same as if you said, 'No proof has been found that X is a cardsharp.' But the confiscation of such a denial was difficult, the official censor of the State Press Bureau had to assume it had come either from the Corps Commander or from one of the Ministries in Vienna.[5]

So how could he have been so sure that there was any truth behind those rumours? What made him take the risk of going public with such serious allegations? According to Kisch, it had all started with a football match. In those days he was chairman of the second-rate football club Sturm, the only German group that would play against a Czech team. The Sunday game against Union Holeschowitz was an important one, as its outcome decided the club's championship prospects. The team relied heavily on their right back, a man called Hans Wagner, a locksmith by profession. But he never turned up. Sturm lost the match, and Kisch was furious.

Wagner turned up the next day in Kisch's office and explained his absence:

'I was already dressed to go when a soldier came into our shop and said that someone had to go at once to the army corps headquarters to break open a lock.'

'Don't tell me any lies. Such a job wouldn't take more than five minutes. And we delayed the kickoff for a full hour.'

'It took three hours. I had to break into an apartment, then open up all the drawers and closets. There were two gentlemen from Vienna, one of them must have been a Colonel. They were looking for Russian papers and for photographs of military plans.'

'Whose house was it?'

'I believe it belonged to a General. It was a big apartment, on the second floor.'[6]

Kisch put two and two together. The apartment could only have belonged to suicide victim Alfred Redl. This was a sensation, just what a young promising journalist needed to further his career.

The real name of the locksmith who was called to Redl's flat was Wenzel Kučirek. Kisch's biographer Michael Horowitz reckons that even the football match was pure fiction from the start. Still, Kisch has for a long time been regarded as the discoverer of the 'scandal of the century'. His depiction of the events that eventually led to Redl's death, again reality blurred with fiction, was taken for granted and had a formative influence on numerous other writers and filmmakers – more about this later.

In Vienna the situation changed significantly on 28 May, the day of Alfred Redl's funeral. The initial official statement by the Royal and Imperial Telegraphic News Bureau had proclaimed that the funeral would be attended 'by all high ranking officers in the capital, by all troops off duty, and by the cadets of all nearby military academies'.

Funerals in Vienna played an important part in the city's everyday life, as Otto Friedlaender ironically remembers in his autobiography *Letzter Glanz der Maerchenstadt* (Last Glory of the Fairy Tale City).

> There are plenty of 'funeral amateurs' amongst the population of Vienna who never miss a beautiful funeral. They are busy people as there are so many beautiful funerals every day. Poor people save up all their lives for a splendid funeral with a magnificent lying in state and a gala hearse.[7]

The actual scenario at Vienna Central Cemetery was rather different. Once again *Die Zeit* knew all the details and reported how the crowd reacted with great anger when at 12.50 two men appeared carrying the coffin, one of them casually dressed. Only a handful of family members were present, including Redl's two brothers. The coffin was lifted onto a plain hearse drawn by two horses. Not a single military official turned up, no funeral march, no drum-roll or volleys over the grave escorted the Colonel to his final resting place.

But much to the annoyance of the military leadership, two of the wreaths that were laid originated from their own ranks. One is thought to have been offered by the regiment Redl's brother belonged to, the second one carried a ribbon with the inscription 'The Friend to the

Friend', and displayed the name Major Friedrich Novak. An order was given to remove both wreaths, and the cemetery management obliged.

By now, the press had tasted blood and became unstoppable in their thirst for more. On the day of the funeral the *Prager Tagblatt* quoted *Die Zeit* (so did other papers) and had intended to write in more detail about the Colonel's alleged espionage activities – but it got seized.

The next day the Socialists' *Arbeiterzeitung* (Workers' Newspaper) came up with the headline: 'The Colonel of the General Staff – a Spy?' It refers to the article published by *Die Zeit* and continues: 'If you know about the custom to "kindly invite" officers who have committed serious infamy to shoot themselves in order to avoid a court case and conviction, you will conclude from this description that it must have been the same in Redl's case.'

And it went on: if he really was a spy, he clearly must have worked for the Russians. And without doubt he would have been 'the most dangerous spy' of all. The journalist gives a long description of Redl's expert appearances at court.

> The way he talked about all things military showed that he had absolute trust in his own knowledge. You got the impression he really knew what he was talking about. The second expert looked like an utter fool compared to Redl. If they really had managed to buy such a gifted Officer of the general staff, who was highly experienced in both theory and practice of espionage and had the best career prospects, this was surely one of the biggest oddities that had ever emerged from militarism.

And he finishes: 'the mighty military officials will surely realise that it is now too late to try to cover things up or deny the truth'.[8]

The 'mighty officials' had already got the message. Also on 29 May they issued an official communiqué. Redl had 'committed suicide after proven acts of grave misconduct: 1. Homosexual intercourse that led to financial problems. 2. Sale of secret official documents to agents of foreign powers.'

The one-horse cabs (Einspaenner or Comfortables) have 1–3 seats; those with a pair of horses (Fiaker) have either two seats only (known as Zweisitzer) or four seats (known as Viersitzer). There are also Taximeter Cabs and Taximeter Motor Cabs. The 'fiakers' have rubber tyres and drive at a good pace. (Baedeker, *Austria-Hungary*, 1911)

On 30 May the *Prager Tagblatt* joked: the mobilisation plans of the 8th Army Corps had disappeared. Redl had been so upset about this that he committed suicide . . .

Of course, the crucial questions behind these lines are: which secrets had he betrayed to the enemy? And why on earth had the commission allowed the accused to take the truth to his grave? There was perfectly good reason to assume that the main reason behind the 'generous permission' that had been granted to the Colonel was the attempt to cover up the scandal the army officials knew would hit them like a storm. 'So let's play the comedy about the knightly atonement! Then nobody will ever know anything about the embarrassing story, and the rabble of civilians won't get disrupted in their belief in all things military.' And: 'Don't even think about approaching the army with frankness. If you want to talk about the army you have to do so bright-eyed and with passion ... appearance everywhere and at all times is all that counts in Austria.'[9]

In Redl's case, the officials had acted like amateurs and foolishly harmed their own cause. They had allowed the man who'd had the most intimate knowledge of the Empire to escape. Not only did they not know what he had told the enemy, or even who the enemy was. Unfortunately, they had also failed to find out who his collaborators were. The latter were left undisturbed in their midst. And of course, there was a good chance that the clever spy had also sold military secrets of the German Reich – not exactly a trivial matter.

It finally dawned on them that they had messed things up badly. They had to come up with a new story to save their necks. And so they did, through the *Fremdenblatt*, their unofficial voice. They produced the story that, part authentic, part fabricated, became legendary and got replicated in a range of variations throughout the twentieth century in film and literature.[10]

In this new version, poor old Redl appeared as the victim of 'moral misconduct'. All this unspeakable behaviour had of course happened a long time ago, when he was a young man. There were people who knew of the poor young chap's sins, and started to blackmail him. Even one of his own servants was said to have been one of them. He was only a Captain when his debts started to get out of hand, and Redl was worried that this would cost him his career. When he was almost completely crushed a helping hand appeared – an agent from a foreign power.

Redl couldn't resist. He became one of their most valuable spies ever. They also threatened to tell his secret, should he not satisfy their demands. Needless to say, his superiors had harboured serious suspicions. Certain military measures that had only been at planning stage started to get implemented by neighbouring powers. And not only did Redl suddenly appear debt-free, he started to lead a rather luxurious life, binge drinking champagne, pocketing 100,000 Austrian kronen in the last winter alone and driving two expensive automobiles. If anybody asked he replied that he had inherited the money.

Our clever superiors decided it was now time for a trap. They sent a false invitation that invited him to Vienna, to meet an agent they assumed was one of his contacts. Redl acted immediately, travelled to the capital in his own automobile, accompanied by a servant, and checked into a first-class hotel.

So far so good; now he left his own car at the hotel to meet the agent. The authorities checked the car and conveniently found: a Browning pistol, a case for a pocket knife and scraps of paper. Redl had already been slightly worried when the agent had not turned up at the agreed place. It got much worse when he returned to his hotel. Although he was in civilian clothes, a stranger awaited him with the case for his knife and the words: 'Colonel Redl, you left this in your car.' He immediately assumed that this stranger was a police agent and that the car had been searched.

He found four officers waiting outside his room. They confronted him with the accusations and the unpleasant news that enough proof had already been discovered in Redl's Prague domicile. The officers then left him to it, and Redl left the hotel, though only for a short while and, of course, under close surveillance. Two officers stayed in the hotel. When Redl returned between 8pm and 9pm, he found on his table a Browning (not his own) and an instruction booklet for the same, just in case the Colonel had forgotten how to handle firearms.

Whoever had placed it there had kindly left it open on the page that describes how to pull the trigger. Dutifully, he instantly decided to commit suicide. He wrote several farewell letters, each annotated with the hour it had been composed. At 4am the servant was asked to check on his master. He found him lying in a pool of blood. He had killed himself at about 2am in front of the mirror. Nobody had heard the shot, not even the couple and their daughter next door, who only woke up when they heard the servant screaming for help. He constantly questioned how his master had acquired the Browning as it wasn't his own. The officers and police agents left the hotel when news reached them. Soon afterwards a military commission arrived and seized everything they found in the room.

This material was perfect for a writer like Kisch. He combined the stories, changed the course of action here and there and embellished it with dramatic details. The following excerpts have been taken from his fourth and last adaption, published in his books *Prager Pitaval* and *Marktplatz der Sensationen* (Sensation Fair):

> Early in the year 1913 two letters reached the general delivery department of Vienna's main Post Office. Both letters carried the identifying cypher 'Opera Ball 13', typed out on a machine. They had been posted at Eydtkuhnen, a town on the German-Russian border. These letters aroused a certain suspicion, all the more so when they were opened and found to contain Austrian banknotes – six thousand Kronen in one, eight thousand in the other (…).
>
> Two Secret Service men, Ebinger and Steidl, were dispatched to the Post Office, to keep a constant watch. They

had a room connected electrically with the general delivery wicket, so if anyone called for the letters they could be immediately notified by the employee in charge of that window, who had simply to ring a bell. (…)

On the evening of May 24, 1913, a Saturday, five minutes before the official closing hour, the bell began to ring in the room of the Secret Service men, stirring them out of their accustomed calm. Before they could reach the general delivery window, where the employee had taken as long as he could without arousing undue suspicion on the part of the receiver, the latter had already taken his 'Opera Ball' letters and left.

They hurried after the man and were able to catch a glimpse of a portly gentleman slamming shut the door of a taxicab just as it rolled away from the curb where it had been parked. … But now, for both of them and for the Austrian army as well, there began a whole series of incredible coincidences, sheer blind luck.

The two police agents stood on the Kolowat Ring and debated with themselves. Should they chase up the driver at once and invent some fairy tale about a hot chase in which the quarry had nevertheless made a getaway? (…) While they were still trying to make up their minds, they blinked; for there, suddenly, was the taxi which twenty minutes before had carried off their prize. The very same number; they signalled, they whistled, they screamed, they gave chase. The taxi stopped. It was empty.

The detectives decide to board the vehicle and follow the unknown individual through Vienna. In the interior of the cab they find: 'a case or sheath for a pocketknife, made of light grey cloth. (…)'. Their chase ends at the hotel Klomser where Steidl instructs the porter to find out which of the guests the case belongs to. Down the stairs comes Redl, '… in uniform, buttoning his gloves'. He stops at the desk and lays down the key to room Number One. In the telephone booth meanwhile Detective Ebinger is reporting that by coincidence Colonel

Redl is also stopping at the Klomser. Should they report to the Colonel? 'Is it possible that the spy may have purposely taken the room here in order to get close to the Colonel?'

'Did you happen to lose the case to your knife?' the porter asks Colonel Redl, while in the booth opposite, Ebinger is telling his chief what they found in the taxi. 'Yes,' says Colonel Redl, and taking his knife out of his pocket he slips it into the light grey case, 'I've been missing it for the last fifteen minutes. Where did you find – '

In the midst of his question he stops, for he knows the answer. (…) With a sudden jerk he turns around and notices a man who seems to be making a great show of being deeply interested in turning over the pages of the register. Colonel Redl knows the man. That was when Colonel Redl turned pale as death, for he knew at once that he was a dead man.

He stepped out into the street, walked away rapidly. (…) Meanwhile the two Secret Service men are still on Redl's tail. They catch sight of him in a passageway. And he too catches sight of them. He tears up papers and throws the bits on the floor. He thinks that one of the detectives will stop to gather up the shreds, and it will be easier then to slip away from the other. (…)

These scraps of paper were conveyed at once to the Board of Investigation where they were put together. They turned out to be postal receipts for money orders sent to a lieutenant in the Uhlans (lancers) at Stockerau, and for registered letters sent to Brussels, Warsaw and Lausanne. (…)

In the Klomser Hotel, just a few hours before, Colonel Redl had received a visit from Lieutenant Stefan Hromadka, an officer in the Uhlans at Stockerau, and as pretty as a picture. They had had a long discussion over their friendship, which the dear boy wished to break up in order to marry. At half-past five Lieutenant Hromadka had left, and ten minutes later Colonel Redl stepped out in order to go to the Post Office to claim his money. He had been putting the matter off for weeks because there was a certain amount of risk involved. But now he had no choice. He had promised Stefan an auto. He thought that if the two of them were to take a long cross-country trip together, the separation of Stefan from his fiancée might make him forget his intention to marry.

In the meantime, Colonel Urbanski von Ostrymiecz, who led the Board of Investigation, reported to the Head of the General Staff, General Conrad von Hoetzendorf.

'Spit it out, August! I'm prepared for the worst.'

'Your Excellency, the man is Colonel Redl.'

'Who, are you mad?' Hoetzendorf exclaimed. 'Are you trying to make a fool of me?' (…) General Conrad von Hoetzendorf had sunk into his chair and was holding both hands against his heart. (…)

'That wretch must die at once!'

(…)

At midnight four high ranking officers appear at the Hotel Klomser. They knock at the door of room Number One. A hoarse 'Come in' is heard and the quartet step inside. Colonel Redl is seated at his table and twice makes an effort to rise but each time falls back in his chair. Finally he stands, swaying. 'I know why you gentlemen have come,' he manages to say. (…)

The commission asks Redl about his accomplices.

'I have none,' he replies.

'Who induced you to become a spy?'

'The Russian military attaché in Vienna, he forced me – because he found out – that – that I am – a homosexual.'

The four officers shiver with disgust; (…)

The General: 'You may request a weapon, Herr Redl.'

Redl: 'I – humbly – request a – revolver.'

(…)

The detective who was called up at five o'clock in the morning was Ebinger. He was ordered to go up to Colonel

13

Redl's room. (…) A few minutes later Ebinger reported to the commission, 'The room was not locked. I opened the door. Colonel Redl was lying dead near the sofa.'

Urbański von Ostrymiecz went to Prague and reported to Baron Giesl, the Commanding Officer of the Army Corps. After lunch they went to Redl's apartment. It was locked and no one had a duplicate key. And while the commission is standing in front of this locked door, I am standing on the football field of Holleschowitz. Our match is scheduled to begin, but our ending, Wagner, has not arrived.[11]

This last sentence alone exemplifies nicely how the journalist Kisch likes to give way to the fiction writer. The locksmith on duty was in fact called Wenzel Kučirek, and he had not been called to deal with the front door, as Giesl did produce a second key. Instead, he had been called to open a number of cases endowed with 'English' (Chubb) locks. The large numbers of discrepancies led Kisch's biographer Michael Horowitz to believe that the whole football match was pure invention.

While Kisch developed his own popularity – he was soon celebrated internationally as a 'young wonder journalist' who managed to solve one mystery after another – his colleagues kept spinning new theories, more or less independently from official directions, that turned up one day and were forgotten the next. One stronger strand was a new idea on how to shift the blame: surely, a woman had her finger in the pie? The same papers that had just declared Redl's homosexuality jumped on the same bandwagon and published detailed articles. Redl was said to have had affairs with glamorous ladies, and especially one long-lasting relationship with a 'certain very elegant' one, who was of course in fact a spy and sent him to his doom. Even the *Fremdenblatt* took the same line. The woman was Russian, incredibly beautiful and sent to Vienna with the one and only mission to lure him into her trap.

Reasonable journalists kept criticising and questioning the fairy tales and urged their readers not to lose sight of the real issues, mainly the failure of those responsible in the army. The *Arbeiterzeitung* wrote, 'the whole world is asking, are they blind or did they simply choose not to care?' The Russians knew that Redl was deep in debt, his own colleagues didn't? They blindly believed in his simple explanation that he had inherited some money.

Quite a bit of money – in 1906 he owned four horses and kept them in his own stables. It seemed that he had started trading them, as new horses kept arriving, allegedly from Galicia and Russia, while others disappeared. Redl led a life of luxury, he ended up with four servants and a chauffeur (all of whom enjoyed a pleasant lifestyle themselves), two expensive cars, a high-quality furnished flat, and spent his spare time binge-drinking champagne.

The conclusion was: 'There was only one clever guy in the General Staff, unfortunately he happened to be a spy. Judas sacrificed one person, (…) Redl was prepared to trap hundreds of thousands of Austrian and German soldiers. A paid gangster almost became Europe's fate.'[12] In the meantime his collaborators and blackmailers remained free to roam. Not a single arrest had been made and what about those mysterious women, or his male sexual partners?

The officials had to show results. So they did. They questioned a sophisticated woman, a foreigner, once married to an Austrian but now divorced, she was said to have had an affair with Redl for eight years. Still, no one saw a reason to keep her in custody. Instead, all eyes moved what was believed to be the bigger catch: the Lieutenant Stephan Horinka from the 7th Galician Uhlan Regiment was arrested, in his (female) lover's flat (paid for by Russia).

He had been seen in Redl's company for several years, so frequently that he was believed to be his son, although Redl used to introduce him as his nephew. Needless to say that he was neither. Together they enjoyed la dolce vita to the full. In the days before his arrest Horinka had appeared restless to his neighbours. Now that he was confined no one knew what the charges actually were – did they concern his homosexuality, or was he also accused of being a spy?

The only official statement, published in the *Militaerische Rundschau* on 1 June concerned the 'outrageous' rumours that Redl had passed on mobilisation and deployment plans to the enemy. 'As anyone who is sufficiently knowledgeable about military organisations knows – no officer is in the position to pass on military secrets to foreign powers.' But surely Redl wasn't your ordinary officer?

The official denial was believed to be mainly directed towards Germany, and Berlin sent the conciliatory reply that no harm had been done: although the relations with their neighbour were excellent, this kind of material would never be brought to the attention of any foreign power.

But a semi-official article unearthed another attempt to relieve the army officials from being accused of failure: they now claimed that Redl had made a full confession before he died. He had provided detailed information about when he had started, who he had worked for and what he had sold them. And he gave the names of other officers involved, strange though that, with the exception of Horinka, no arrests were heard of. One journalist joked: 'Good for them that it's now in the papers, it will remind them that it's time to flee.'

Redl's case also made it into Parliament. Several questions and interpellations concerned mainly two areas: why was he allowed or even forced to commit suicide? And how come Generaladvokat (assistant to the general procurator) Pollak, a judicial official, had been part of the commission that had allowed the accused to skip legal proceedings? The Defence Minister promised to come up with answers within a week's time.

In the meantime, in these early days of June 1913, countless different stories about Redl's life and career circulated in the papers, amongst them a considerable amount of what would have been slander, had he been alive. It was said that he had accused his own brother, also an officer, of being a spy. To disable Austrian espionage in Russia, he had declared Austrian spies to Russian spies. Civilian clothes were found beside Redl's dead body – proof that he had planned an escape. All that was missing from the big picture was clarity.

And clarity was certainly not achieved by the statement that was finally given by the Defence Minister Freiherr von Georgi on 5 June, based on information provided by the ministers of war and of justice, 'the most embarrassing moment of his long career'.

According to Georgi, there had been indications of espionage for quite a while, and Redl had been under surveillance. On 24 May they finally had proof. On the very same day Redl arrived in Vienna and went for dinner with Generaladvokat Pollak. He told his old friend that he had committed a crime against morality and professional honour, but did not give any details. He knew he was under surveillance and asked Pollak to lend him a revolver.

Pollak refused. Redl changed course and requested his help to gain permission to return to Prague. This Pollak promised to arrange, and went to make a phone call to the Head of Police Edmund von Gayer. Instead of acting on Redl's request, he asked for advice on how to deal with the officer who seemed confused and made no sense to him. Maybe he could be admitted to a psychiatric hospital? Gayer thought the best thing to do would be to try and calm the man down, and ask him to return to his hotel. This plan succeeded.

The Minister emphasised repeatedly that Pollak was not part of the commission that came to visit Redl at the hotel, nor had he been involved in any decision-making. At 10pm the Chief of the General Staff had officially established Redl's guilt and went on to form a commission. This took until midnight, when they set off to Redl's hotel where they arrived at 12.30. They had also been informed by the police about Pollak's phone call and Redl's announcement that he wanted to shoot himself.

They found the accused in his room with a cord lying on his bed and a dagger on his desk. He welcomed them with the words: 'I know why the gentlemen are here. I feel guilty.' During the interrogation Redl admitted to espionage but insisted that he had no accomplices, that no one knew his real identity and that he had only been involved in espionage for a short time. Satisfied with his answers, the commission left him to it. The hotel remained under surveillance to prevent his escape. The next day he was found dead in his room.

Delegate Leuthner: 'So where did he get the revolver from, or can you shoot yourself with a cord?'

Minister: 'The commission did not order the Colonel's suicide, which he had evidently already planned, nor did it force him to commit it.'

Delegate Hillebrand: 'They should have prevented it!'

Minister: 'On 25 May we searched Colonel Redl's flat and his office in Prague. His paperwork showed that he had indeed been a spy, but also that he had homosexual relations, in particular and for some time to one Lieutenant, the so-called nephew, and that this confusion had without doubt led to high levels of spending. The detailed notes they had found in Prague provided proof that his confession in Vienna was true and complete.'

Leuthner: 'But you did not arrest him!'

Minister: 'All available data indicates that he began spying in March 1912. We have to state with deep regret that Redl has indeed passed on general instructions related to the mobilisation of the armed forces to foreign powers.'

Delegate Nemec: 'Powers! That's important!'

Minister: 'Despite the gravity of this fact it has to be noted that specific recent measures (deployment plans) could not have been given away as they could not have been accessed by Redl.

With regards to Redl's obvious high spending I have to say: the big expenditure is without doubt a result of him satisfying his unnatural passions; obviously the way this money was spent remained hidden from the public and could not attract attention. Redl explained the efforts that resulted from the acquisition of expensive horses, the keeping of expensive cars etc. with an inheritance of which he ostentatiously told people around him. There was indeed a certificate of inheritance amongst the paperwork, but only a small amount of this inheritance that was shared out between many heirs was allocated to Redl.

There are actually a number of indicators that point towards serious debt, this is currently being investigated, and it seems like this debt increased daily, despite him having led a more modest life in the recent more critical days compared to his past.

As seen above, it has so far been established that Redl's espionage goes back to March 1912. It can therefore be assumed impossible that he started many years ago.

Especially during the many years he was employed by the Evidenzbureau, where he frequently acted as an expert on espionage, his position speaks against the possibility of having played an active part as an agent for a foreign power, as Redl had always shown a rigid approach in cases of espionage ...'

Delegate Habermann: 'The goat as the gardener!'

Minister: '... and would have risked betrayal by these agents.

No accomplices were found. I have to add it would have made little sense for someone so accomplished with the techniques of espionage to burden himself with accomplices that could have turned into a danger for him at any given time.

The Lieutenant we mentioned earlier got arrested, but he is so far not suspected of espionage. Rumours that higher ranking officers as well as a lady had been compromised were proven wrong. A connection between Redl and the Russian Consul in Prague could not be established. There is no connection to the Jandrić or other recent cases of espionage. All rumours of Redl having sold secrets about the German army are wrong; the same applies to assertions made by the press that Colonel Redl had been sent to meetings with the German General Staff.

Our magnificent and glorious army got hit hard when an unworthy desecrated its honour. But one person's disgrace cannot affect a whole community and its countless examples of boundless self-sacrifice, the highest sense of duty and heroism. I'm therefore not worried that just because of this one mishap our army could lose people's trust, which means a lot to us, or that it could lose the respect of foreign armies, the former we will always justify and try to earn, the latter, if necessary, enforce.'

The minister's speech earned no applause at all. Delegate Nemec proposed a debate, but this was rejected by the governing parties. Later on that day, during a budget debate, Social Democrat Seitz took his chance to criticise the minister for a speech full of bad stylistic blunders, but short of facts. It was still a mystery who had ordered Redl to come to Vienna. Why was he allowed to roam the city when it was clear that he was a spy?

What if he used that time to warn his accomplices? What if Pollak himself was one of them? The commission listens to his confession but still doesn't arrest him. Instead the culprit is left by himself in his room with cord and dagger. Hours later they return and find him dead. Who gave him the Browning? If it hadn't been the commission, why wasn't the police looking into this? How could they possibly take the confession of this highly agitated man seriously? Why did they not initiate criminal proceedings?

Instead, leaving the cord behind reminds one of the most primitive days of justice, the 'silk thread of the Turkish sultans'. [Turkish sultans sent a silk thread to high-ranking personalities who were sentenced to death. The condemned was then usually strangled by a servant or soldier. Through this method the sultans could get rid of relatives to secure their rule, without shedding their royal blood; occasionally, the convicted 'were allowed' to escape the strangling by suicide.] According to the minister there were no accomplices?

Who transferred the money, who received his telegrams? What about the mysterious ladies? And the foreign powers, they paid millions without even knowing the guy? The only country that could possibly be that naïve would be Austria itself! If the minister accepts the claim that Redl had not engaged in espionage before March 1912, it only proves that there was never a proper interrogation, nor a serious investigation, or that he covers up the real facts. And what happened to the tax man? Any ordinary man gets harassed if he kicks over the traces, surely Redl's permanent excesses would have led to some questioning? But why ask if all you want to do is hide the truth?

The minister desperately seeks our trust – but it is not just the Social Democrats – whoever is capable of reasonable thought amongst the middle classes will tell him that his elaborations have ruined the trust in the army leadership as well as in the government. The main virtues commonly praised in soldiers were missing completely: bravery and truthfulness.[13]

The Defence Minister's official statement, disappointing as it was, also formed a turning point in public reporting. Newspaper articles became shorter and rarer. The press focused on more pressing issues. Less than a month after the Treaty of London is signed at an international conference of Europe's ambassadors, to settle the First Balkan War, the second one erupts when Bulgaria, disgruntled about the outcome of the previous conflict, attacks its former allies Serbia and Greece.

At the same time a young disillusioned artist called Adolf Hitler leaves Vienna, where he had several times failed to gain admission to the Academy of Fine Arts, to settle down in the German Fatherland, but is tracked down by the Austrian authorities and faces with the possibility of prison for avoiding military service.

And the Archduke Franz Ferdinand declares plans to inspect Habsburg troops in Bosnia in 1914.

Alfred Redl's real story remained a mystery. In some ways it still remains so today. But let us turn the clock back to the year 1864, when the family of a railway clerk in Lemberg, Galicia, was about to expand …

Chapter 2

The Boy from Lemberg

To begin with, the Austrian is a willing and hard working individual, and since industry is the blessing of men, this excellent characteristic has preserved him from downfall. But the Austrian has none of that assiduity which makes the German apply himself with the sole object of making money. No, money-making is the last aim of the Austrian. He has far too much of the artist's temperament, he works for the work's sake and possesses the big, generous heart of the true artist. (Countess Landi)

Everything in our almost thousand-year-old Austrian Monarchy seemed based on permanency, and the state itself was the chief guarantor of this stability. The rights which it granted to its citizens were duly confirmed by parliament, the freely elected representatives of the people, and every duty was exactly prescribed ... (Stefan Zweig)

In Dino Buzzati's 1940 novel *The Tartar Steppe*,[1] the hero Drogo is an officer assigned to a vast decaying fortress on the edge of a nameless desert, the void of anarchy which stretches limitlessly eastwards. This great crumbling bulwark is manned by a forgotten garrison whose whole existence is spent waiting for the barbarian horde to emerge. The themes of the book and the 1976 film adaptation *Desert of the Tartars*[2] are those of the need to serve and desperate yearning for the balm of glory. Alfred Redl has something of this character in him, the need to belong to a particular caste – the officer caste which elevates a man from the ordinary, a civilian into the elite, the brotherhood of arms, a badge of gentility.

Yet Drogo gains nothing from his long vigil, other than a creeping unnamed malady that seems to emanate from the very stones and, when the attack finally comes, he is too ill to stand on the ramparts. Behind the sandstone bulk of the castle, life in the garrison town continues as a civilised norm. This scenario could be an analogy for the last half century of the Austro-Hungarian army, the ragged banners of six centuries of tradition finally being engulfed by the rising certainty of industrial war; a new breed of conflict that turns battle into a firestorm from which none of the old certainties will ever emerge.

Alfred Redl was born on 14 March 1864, three years before the creation of the Dual Monarchy and at a time when Prussia, the new leader of Germany, was already flexing her formidable might against the unprepared Danes. Austria's nemesis as the dominant force in the Teutonic world came not out of the anonymous steppe but from Bismarck in Berlin. Alfred's family lived in the ancient fortress city of Lemberg.[3] The 'City of the Lion' stands in western Ukraine, formerly the capital of the largely forgotten and wonderfully archaic Kingdom of Ruthenia. In 1339 this was subsumed into the rising Polish state, the regional capital of the Ruthenian Voivodeship.[4] It was not until 1772, when Poland was sliced apart, that it came into Habsburg hands, becoming the administrative centre of Galicia and Lodomeria.

Lemberg had been an economic and cultural centre for 650 years when Franz Redl moved his family there. Theirs was not a prosperous existence. Franz worked as an Expeditor second class,[5] a minor logistics role for his employer, the Carl Ludwig Railway. For this he received a woollen uniform and 700 gulden a year in wages,[6] a modest salary for a man with numerous mouths to feed. Despite such a humble post in a distant provincial city, Franz Redl had once been an officer and had served for eleven years as a lieutenant. In the Great War, British territorial officers who served on the Western Front, the 'Saturday Night Soldiers' of pre-war derision, would gain the dubious status of 'temporary gentlemen'; officers during hostilities but with a drop in social standing on their return to Civvy Street.

The army whilst always prestigious was made up of a complex layer cake of hierarchies (see Chapter 4). The cavalry formed the cream and it was said that an aspiring cadet would have to show he'd sixteen generations of gentry ancestors behind him before he stood a chance of selection and even here nobility were distinguished from mere gentry. Franz wasn't quite a gentleman. He was lower middle class and thus consigned to the infantry where social strata were less rigidly interpreted.

His service marched in time with the glories of Radetzky and he'd left before the blood-garnished humbling of the battles of Magenta and Solferino. Austrian society, like most, established a clear fault line between the soldier and the civilian, der Civilist. Traditionally, the man in uniform was always a cut above and an eligible groom for aspiring young women. And that proved to be the problem. An officer could not marry unless his prospective father-in-law could deposit the necessary funds as a dowry or *Kaution*. For a junior lieutenant the price of nuptials came rather high and in Franz's case, it seems his wife Mathilde's father simply couldn't come up with the cash.

So Franz had stopped being a gentleman and become a state employee, working for the railroad on 500 gulden per annum. After seven years of marriage and now with four children to feed, he was only 200 gulden a year better off. When the Carl Ludwig Company, a private consortium, came along with a better offer, he couldn't afford to refuse. For the following five years he and his family moved around Galicia as the company dictated before being finally posted on a more permanent basis to Lemberg.

It might not be Vienna, indeed it was very far from the imperial heartland, a chunk of what had been Poland ruthlessly carved up nearly a century beforehand. The city lies nearly 160 km from the eastern Carpathians, the mountain barrier that separates heartlands from frontier. Yet it wasn't as though Lemberg (the German spelling) had done badly out of the annexation, quite the opposite, the place had boomed.

The old, medieval core clustered around the base of the castle mound by the banks of the River Poltva, the conduit for trade and growth, had at the time of the acquisition a population of no more than 30,000. By the time Alfred was born this had increased at least six-fold. Bureaucracy creates jobs and the Habsburgs certainly did bureaucracy. Increasingly, the ancient eastern character of the old town was subsumed beneath a gloss of Austrian baroque: opulent squares and a rash of coffee houses, influences which survive today throughout Galicia. Visitors to the beautiful and vast plaza which is Krakow's historic square can be forgiven for thinking they're in Vienna or Budapest.

The upheavals of 1848 had, at least in part, halted the enforced Germanisation of Galicia, Ukrainian and Polish were again admitted as the languages of academia and culture. Lemberg was the first imperial city to be illuminated by kerosene street lighting in 1853 and the advent of the Dual Monarchy led to a steadily increasing degree of liberalism and autonomy. The Poles and their votes were needed to balance the Magyar influence so the local authority or Sejm was relatively pampered. This cultural mix was extremely vibrant. Both the opera and ballet houses were built, in florid Viennese style, statements of confidence and artistic expression. Some of the glory that was Vienna travelled out to the provinces and mingled easily with the native style. Probably nobody thought then it might end and that the day may not be that far off. Habsburg rule, even if it was a form of tyranny, was enforced with a lighter touch. After 1914 and the vicissitudes of total war, far worse would follow.

Traditionally, the city housed a substantial Jewish community who comprised some 28 per cent of the population. A majority, just over half, were Catholic. Polish was the dominant language with only 11 per cent speaking Ukrainian. Despite the Habsburg/German dominance and regardless of the sops to national and local identity, Polish nationalism was far from quiescent. Such future lions as Pilsudski,[7] Sikorski[8] and Sosnkowski[9] were, by the early twentieth century, organising Polish paramilitaries. Yet, at the same time Lemberg was a focal point for the Ukrainians. A number of distinguished and popular authors were published there, cultural institutions and groups flourished. Poles and Ukrainians rubbed along with the Jews whose own individual culture was equally lively. Lemberg was a world-class centre for studies of Yiddish and the *Lemberger Togblat* was the world's first daily paper printed in the language.

Alfred Redl was born into this cosmopolitan goulash. His family were Austro-Hungarian and his father's past service offered some level of kudos above the mundane role he now played. The family was poor but they were not paupers. Franz had a secure job and working for the railways had at least some minor cachet. Mathilde seems to have been from Magyar stock, which after 1867 implied a greater level of equality. They were not impoverished gentry; merely impoverished, they lacked position and connection. Life wasn't desperate but it was without variety, spice or aspiration. For a young man seeking all of these, it had little going for it.

Provincial Lemberg might be doing very well, yet the contrast between those who had position and wealth, many drawn from the old Polish gentry classes, and those who didn't would be galling to many and perhaps especially to a boy born with wit and ambition.

The Imperial Governor at the time [1869] was Count Goluschowski. He was very rich and felt himself more an Imperial Satrap than Governor – more an assistant king than a high official. Under such auspices the Polish influence became strongly dominant and the German upper-class society as well as the Ruthenian lower-class society was soon completely pushed to the side.[10]

Despite a persistent undercurrent of nationalism and echoes of anti-Semitism always just beneath the surface, Lemberg was not necessarily the brooding hotbed of conspiracy and discontent that Robert Asprey suggests. For all its contradictions and its many defeats, the Empire appeared to offer permanence. Lemberg might be provincial but it was far from parochial or insular: the arts flourished.

What guided Alfred's childhood was near poverty. He was the fourth of nine children and even though Franz's wages had gone up to 2,400 gulden, that was a lot of clamouring mouths.[11]

Like all of his contemporaries, the young Alfred Redl would attend his local *Volksschule* (literally, 'people's school'). This form of combined primary and early stage secondary education was compulsory for all, a long-established German tradition, going back certainly as far as the seventeenth century.[12] He was clearly quick-witted and perhaps his daily journey to school past those florid baroque facades of the city's busy centre fuelled that steel core of ambition which would drive him so relentlessly.

If you or your family weren't affluent, provincial life was pretty mundane. Summer trips to the hills, mass on Sundays. Robert Asprey suggests that he escaped from the dullness of his overcrowded home life by developing an early sense of dream-fuelled aspiration and that he hid his quickness behind a mask of dull conformity. This may be true, perhaps even likely, but he was certainly quick at school and could take refuge from the teeming, tedious warren of home in fanciful dreams. Whether he regularly fantasised about an opulent, upper middle class lifestyle, one with servants and crystal and carriages, we cannot ever say but it's by no means impossible. His later fondness for ostentation would certainly suggest that he did.

There was one glimmer, a potent flicker in the drab greyness. Every year Franz took Alfred and his brother Heinrich to watch the annual military manoeuvres. Now here was colour, the dazzling uniforms, officers' heavy with braid, venerable shot-torn banners that resonated with echoes of Napoleonic glory. Despite their reduced circumstances, the middle-aged Franz, ground down, shabby, insignificant, was still a part of this, some shreds of distant chivalry still clung to his lumpen worker's outfit, a reminder to Alfred that his father, however temporarily, had been a gentleman. This was the escape route.

At the age of 55, Franz Redl escaped the monotony of his post-gentlemanly life. He died of purely natural causes, worn down by the treadmill – although some papers would later claim that he committed suicide. To what extent Alfred was affected by his father's death we can't really say. They do not appear to have been close. Perhaps it did affect him to the extent he wanted something better, not the life-draining monotony of material failure. Franz left his grieving widow and all of his many children to exist on a modest widow's pension. The railway company did provide – the family weren't destitute but their poverty just got worse. Whatever modest savings Franz and Mathilde had amassed were gobbled up by funeral expenses. By now there were ten children under 18 and living at home. For Alfred, no escape route had opened up as he moved to secondary or *Realschule* (usually for ages 11–16/17).

For three years he attended, studied hard, impressed his teachers, chafing at the domestic dominance of bossy older sisters who seemed to rule the household, Ernestine, Helena and Ottilia. In 1877, older sibling Oskar escaped the provincial blues by getting into cadet school. Two years later Alfred followed the same route, even though he was only 14. The entrance exams proved no great hurdle and he got into Karthaus Cadet School situated in his home town in the autumn of 1879. As his father had previously served, there were no fees to pay. His life was about to change.

The military academy is simply an educational establishment dedicated to preparing students for service in their country's armed forces. The trend had developed during the Age of Reason and it had been Empress Maria Theresa who had established the first such school in 1751. Her Theresan Military Academy is a world-class institution to this day. Frederick the Great and Napoleon had elevated the art of war to a more precise science. Officers in mass armies needed to know their business, rather than muddle through as more or less dedicated amateurs with a family history behind them.

Military schools have perhaps not enjoyed a good press. *Maedchen in Uniform*, a 1931 screen version of Christa Winsloe's play portrays the female equivalent in a most unflattering light, Do-the-Boys' Hall in uniform. Alfred Redl, on the other hand, had no complaints. Wearing uniforms, all cut from the same anonymous broad-cloth, is a great leveller. If the kit doesn't yet make you a gentleman, it marks you immediately out from the non-uniformed civilian. An elite tradition follows you, *trailing clouds of glory,* echoes of Thermopylae and Roncesvalles. For him Karthaus was never a prison, more a seminary, where the initiates strove to become worthy. His father had been an officer and that was sufficient cachet for the moment.

Alfred had always been a keen student, the apt pupil hungry for the salve of praise. A military curriculum suited him; there was precision, the mathematics of war, use of ground, calculating ranges, lines of sight and of fire. The army of Austria-Hungary had suffered some telling defeats but it proved both resilient and capable of changing. It was an exciting time. Austria was not the only nation learning how to live with humiliation. France had experienced far worse in 1870–1, her armies humbled and passed beneath the Prussian yoke, Paris besieged, Alsace and Lorraine stripped and appropriated by the conquerors. As a loser you need to learn, only the victor can rest, probably only briefly, on his amassed laurels.

Germany and the Kaiser's General Staff system provided the new benchmark. Bismarck and von Moltke had revolutionised war in the same way Frederick had done a century earlier. Germany's military might was fuelled by a rapidly expanding manufacturing economy which was growing at a rate that could challenge the world's only superpower – the British Empire. Britain at this time was friendly towards Germany. Bashing the French was not something that would ever offend the English. The rich travelled and holidayed on the Rhine, drank Mosel and read Goethe. It would take Kaiser Wilhelm's bull-in-a-china-shop diplomacy to change all that.

Wars of the eighteenth century, the days of Frederick and Maria Theresa, were generally directed by an inner political circle within the framework of the emerging state. In German these wars, often dynastic, are described, aptly, as *Kabinettskriege* or 'Cabinet Wars'. These were fought by mainly professional soldiers with limited strategic objectives and, in theory at least, a degree of restraint.[13]

The growth of nationalism in the later eighteenth century and the lessons of the American War of Independence favoured the rise of mass citizen armies. Although, in terms of loss of life, the long era of Napoleonic conflict (1792–1815) was less bloody than the Thirty Years

War (1618–48),[14] the social, political and military changes were much more far-reaching. It was the French Revolutionary minister of war the brilliant Lazare Carnot who first introduced the notion of mass conscription – 'service in the army as part of the patriotic obligations of citizenship, coupled with an attempt to organise the whole of French society for war at the service of the state'.[15]

This new warfare found little time for restraint; French armies, encouraged to live off the land, stripped countries bare like a biblical plague and showed little mercy towards subject populations. These armies were commanded by a new breed – Napoleon's marshals were often men of humble beginnings. The need for larger armies with ever more complex logistical needs created opportunities for hungry and ambitious young men like Alfred Redl. Fighting was no longer the sole province of patricians.

Although he would never be tall, never quite meet the cavalier image of the officer class, Alfred was a tryer. He was quick and he was fit. He could master gymnastics and fencing. Though the sword was long obsolete as a weapon, the mystique of cold steel held good. To be competent with épée and sabre was rather more useful than being a good shot. Anyway, most officers from gentry backgrounds would hunt and thus learn to handle firearms. Most would have scrapped with blades from an early age. It was all new to Alfred but he embraced the culture with gusto. The sword was the badge of rank; officers still carried them (as they do at passing out and ceremonial parades today). Alfred needed to be an officer.

Writing just on the cusp of industrial warfare, Clausewitz in his magisterial work *On War* spelled out the ground rules for the nation wanting to embark on a successful interstate war. He referred to this as his 'trinity': the executive who decided policy, the military who put it into effect and the people in general whose taxes would be paying for the war and whose sons might be expected to put on uniform. His lodestar was the concept of 'primacy of policy' – war could only be successful if the outcome was dictated by a realisable and sustainable political objective.

Alfred Redl was, in many ways, the perfect tool for the age of

Clausewitz, the professional and highly focused officer, driven by the need to impress and to excel, someone who had something to prove rather than a status he'd inherited. In fact, he'd arrived just at the right time. Clausewitz didn't specifically include this but military intelligence was another essential prop. You needed to know what the other fellow was up to. This demanded a very skilled breed of officer, those who were good at it were very few and far apart. Alfred would become the best.

Industry changed the face of war. From the 1840s, railways played an increasingly vital role. Until then, the army moved only as fast as the infantryman could march and the cavalryman could ride. Logistical tails stretched back for miles, vulnerable, unwieldy and unreliable. In 1859, Napoleon III's army relied on trains, moving troops at undreamed of speeds into Northern Italy. Von Moltke's whole *blitzkrieg* against Austria seven years later was predicated on the strategic use of railways. The outcome led to a whole generation of military planners working on how best to use the tracks. By 1914 Germany had over 40,000 miles of it; national railways were laid out as much for military as civilian use.[16]

Although all armies would remain heavily dependent on horsepower until the outbreak of the Great War and indeed up till 1939, motor vehicles became increasingly common after the end of the nineteenth century. Alfred Redl would cause quite a stir when he acquired a sleek and very fashionable automobile. Balloons had been used for observation during earlier wars but the advent of the aircraft would be another game-changer. Armies of the First World War would be badly hampered by lack of short wave radios but communications generally, not just for war itself but as tools in the wider game of espionage, also underwent a revolution during the second half of the nineteenth century. Samuel Morse had perfected his 'Morse Code' in 1837. By 1901 wireless telegraph could send signals across the Atlantic.

Industry didn't just revolutionise the movement of armies or their supply chain. The humble tin can now meant food could be stored for very long periods, avoiding seasonal campaigning. At the same time population levels in the sprawling, insanitary warrens of the great industrial cities grew dramatically. Through the course of the nineteenth century, the peoples of Europe multiplied four-fold. Mass armies need large numbers of recruits, these were now to hand. Getting them into uniform, equipped, mustered, officered, trained and supplied was a major business undertaking in itself

During the war of 1866, Prussia demonstrated that she'd moved on from basic wartime conscription, the mass levy of Bonaparte's day, to a far more sophisticated method of harnessing the nation's youth. Prussia maintained a system of peacetime conscription. Most young men, if physically fit enough, would serve for a couple of years beneath the colours before getting back into civvies. Even then they remained liable for the reserves and a decade's worth of those reserves would be mobilised for war. For the conflict of 1870–1, Prussia was able to field a million soldiers. Nothing on this scale had ever been seen before. A new age needs new men, the rise of a meritocracy, 'temporary gentlemen', would be much in demand and, through hard work and demonstrable zeal, could rise far higher than before.

So the art of war was now an industry and industries need managers. This meant the creation of a highly professional, thoroughly trained and forward-looking General Staff. Their job was to oversee the mobilisation, concentration and supply of the new armies. The battlefield was becoming dominated by firepower. Getting your forces where they needed to be to deliver the firepower at their disposal was becoming key.[17]

Germany led the way, Austria was bound to follow and Alfred Redl intended to be the perfect candidate for this new elite. This was the dazzling prospect history had thrown up. Alfred had neither the lineage nor the means to posture as a *beau sabreur* of the old school; he would have been found out, marked as a fraudster. The new army of mass conscription with a byzantine administrative and technical General Staff at its core was just the stage this actor required. His performance would be sublime.

He would be an officer. His father had attained the status but failed miserably to capitalise on it; Alfred wouldn't make the same mistake.

He was only partly a dreamer, underpinning his hopes was a wide enough streak of ruthless pragmatism and unbridled ambition. For him, the officer corps was the surest route to success. As his father had served, the door was partly open. He could never aspire to an elite cavalry regiment but the infantry was less exclusive.

Besides, there was something about being an officer. The beautifully cut uniforms flaunted their elite wearers, the chasm between soldier and civilian. The Empire had over six hundred years of warrior tradition. An officer could claim cultural and social descent from Hector and Achilles, through the medieval knights of romantic legend, those glorious winged hussars who had seen of the might of the Ottoman hordes before the gates of Vienna. Alfred craved show, he loved to stand out. He yearned to wear the soft doeskin of an officer's tunic, rather than the patched and darned remnants and hand-me-downs of his childhood. An officer had automatic respect, he was *someone*.

Rags of glory have clung to officer status since the Plains of Troy, even in the cynical, post-imperial austerity of the present century:

> Sandhurst had an air of grandeur about it, a certain elegance and even, beyond the shouting and marching, a certain gentility to its stables and polo pitches and black-and-white photographs of back in the day when cadets sporting preposterous moustaches practised bicycle drill.[18]

As well as establishing a clear position in society where inherited wealth, landed or business interest need not be essential, an officer's lifestyle was also his own business. Quite where his resources came from above the fairly meagre salary he might expect wouldn't necessarily excite much comment. If he was discreet, his private life might also be his own affair.

At cadet school Redl strives single-mindedly towards gaining officer status, living a dedicated almost monkish existence like an initiate of one of the knightly orders from the Crusades. Robert Asprey injects some highly speculative comments on the nature of Alfred's homosexuality at this point. Whilst institutions like Karthaus are natural hotbeds for sexual activity, it cannot be said for definite that Alfred necessarily enjoyed his first liaisons here. It may be he did but clearly this was not something that could ever be discussed openly. Homosexual activity was condemned by church and society so inevitably carried out in the shadows. The army was well aware of such occurrences and not necessarily disapproving. Most senior officers realised that their youthful charges required sexual outlets and slaking their desires with each other certainly reduced the high incidence of venereal disease that came in large doses via the brothels.

The fact that he contracted syphilis in 1891 clearly proves that he had sufficient energy for sex of one kind or another though. The illness forced him to take considerable time off school. Still, his track record in academic and sporting studies remained impeccable. After four years hard slog he graduated in 1883, his final assessment came up as 'very good' – not quite excellent but pretty near. He'd already signed up for the regulars over a year before and committed to additional stints in the reserve and home guard echelons. His bounty was 3 gulden, hardly a king's ransom but deemed sufficient for the recruit to buy the basics – a custom that dated back to the Thirty Years War.[19] From then on till he graduated, he was paid the footslogger's meagre rate of 6 kreuzer per day. Having passed out from Karthaus, he was promoted to acting NCO and assigned to the 9th Infantry based in Lemberg.

Robert Asprey interprets Redl's character in a Manichaean, dualist way: 'His evil was forever present in his thoughts. It provided the challenge that his surface existence had to meet. It formed the essence of the life-game that he had to win in order to survive.'[20] This is both simplistic and overly censorious. Alfred Redl was not inherently evil. The consequences of his treachery brought evil upon his nation but to him this was not the intended result. He was reckless of consequences rather than calculating. He was the hub of his own world. His life was his own supreme artistic creation. He was an actor and the murky world of spies and espionage was the absolutely perfect stage.

He was born in Poland but was not Polish. The child of economic migrants might adopt the nationality of domicile but the children of occupiers do not choose, as a rule, to identify with the helots. It is unlikely that any son or daughter of Roman parents born along the length of Hadrian's Wall ever thought of him or herself as one of the despised locals, *Britunculi*. Even where one parent was native, the result was defined by Roman citizenship. Franz and Mathilde as Austrian and Magyar, despite their circumstances, undoubtedly thought of themselves as a significant cut above native Poles or Ukrainians.

Redl would, as an adult, live a parallel existence, not fully in the sense of Descartes, Leibniz or even Jung but his absolute dedication to building the Potemkin village of his life almost precluded the intrusion of reality. He was not only the actor, he was the impresario who built or certainly ingeniously extended the stage he strutted. And he did strut, gleaming, impeccable, inscrutable, known but not known, a generous host, dedicated colleague, one who lived with dash and style and whose means were never seriously questioned.

Perhaps in no time previously could he have hoped to have succeeded. It was the nature of emerging industrial war, the scale and anonymity which provided the base. Alfred consistently worked without respite to master his profession, to shine, to come to the notice of his superiors and to earn good reviews. An actor cannot play to an empty house. His hunger for plaudits craves an audience, one that is prepared readily to applaud and perhaps not look too closely at the props. From his days at school, Alfred liked to earn the praise of his teachers. He needed it, this was fuel and proof the show was working.

By attaining his much coveted position within the General Staff he overcame the lack of blue blood in a single bound. The General Staff formed the ultimate inner circle of the new meritocracy. In 1904, they were no more than four hundred strong out of an officer corps strength of 28,000.[21] As Wellington would have remarked, 'a clique within a caste'.[22] This elevated Redl from mere actor to 'A' list celebrity. Nobody would question him, nobody could scrutinise him. He was above the normal hubbub and intimacies of the traditional mess. He could open doors and then close them behind him, leaving nothing but good opinions.

Like all good fantasy, much was built on solid foundations. He was gifted and bright. He worked unceasingly and showed great intuition. His work in developing the role of military intelligence was revolutionary. His treachery was so well concealed behind a rampart of lies that he escaped detection for as long as he did. It wasn't just success, the constant applause that he sought; he needed the lifestyle to go with it.

Alfred's timing was right not just in terms of the expansion of a professional officer corps but also, even at this twilight stage, in terms of expansion of Empire. This was the age of the 'Scramble for Africa' – Britain, France, Belgium and even Germany, the latecomer, were painting vast national canvases in Africa but not the Dual Monarchy. Her attentions were focused closer to home. Austria bestrode the east–west axis in Europe, partly she faced towards Germany and France but equally she looked east over and towards the Balkans. From the fall of Constantinople in 1453, the Sublime Porte had been the major power in the region, the ancient kingdoms of Serbia and Bulgaria had been swallowed up. By the latter part of the nineteenth century, the Turkish grip had weakened to the point of senility. Bulgaria and Serbia had reasserted themselves as independent Slavic states. Common blood didn't make them friends.

The Russian bear had spread its very sharp claws across Central Asia and now the Tsar saw himself as the natural patriarch of a pan-Slavic brotherhood of lesser nations. This was not to Franz Joseph's liking but after 1905 Russia encountered plenty problems of her own. Defeat at the hands of Japan and internal unrest were more than minor difficulties. There was, for Austria, also the problem of Italy. Nationhood had come at a price for the Empire, stripped of the twin jewels of Lombardy and Venetia. On paper, Italy, Austria and Germany formed the Triple Alliance. Though continually renewed after 1882, this outward show of amity did not decrease suspicion. Italy coveted Trentino and Istria and looked greedily across the Adriatic towards Albania. Her own attempt at African conquest in Ethiopia had ended in humiliation at Adowa. Conrad von Hoetzendorf, the brilliant and bullish commander-in-chief of Austrian armies, was all for pre-emptive strikes against both Italy and Serbia.

Having collided in such a disastrous and bruising war with Japan, Russia, weakened and humiliated, began to contract her ambitions and focus back towards the Balkans. It was only in 1878 that the last Turkish garrisons left Serbia, though she'd been semi-autonomous for decades before. It was the Russian victory over the tottering Ottoman state that won full independence for Serbia. Yet at the outset and for quarter of a century Belgrade looked more towards Vienna than St Petersburg. The disparate and rival mafias which struggled for dominance in Serbia hoped to recover both Macedonia and Albania. Aside from murdering each other, they fixed their general enmity on Bulgaria, itself a client of the Tsar.

Even as late as 1897, Vienna and St Petersburg seemed to be in accord. Both powers agreed to consult over the Balkans and not to go land-grabbing unilaterally – Austria did reserve the right to occupy Bosnia-Herzegovina and the Sanjak of Novibazar.[23] This rapprochement effectively barred the path to any single Balkan state becoming powerful enough to dominate the region. It couldn't last however because the wider battle lines were already being drawn. Germany and Austria, nominally with Italy, were in opposition to France and Russia. Britain was uneasily neutral but 'Kaiser Bill', with his crass championing of the Boers and his rash starting of a naval arms race, alienated Britain and opened the door for the Entente of 1904.

Of the two great central powers, the world viewed Austria as the poor relation. This wasn't necessarily so. As the Kaiser had succeeded in undoing all that Bismarck had achieved, Franz Joseph was left as his only friend. Austria could afford to flex her muscles and her Foreign Minister Count Aehrenthal, appointed in 1906, was determined to do just that. He saw that Austria could expand her influence in the Balkans. Inconveniently, his Russian counterpart Alexander Izvolsky rather thought that Russia might do the same. Rapprochement had just gone out of season.

Aehrenthal was determined to resurrect an imperial alliance between Berlin, Vienna and St Petersburg, 'which would attract France into its orbit and put England and Italy in their places'.[24] He wanted to avoid any sudden resurgence in Ottoman power after the Young Turks had deposed the Sultan.[25] He tried to win over the Serbs and defuse tension between Austrians and Magyars. It was bold and, on the surface, brilliant, but in reality naive and doomed. There was no hope of sidelining Britain, especially once the Russians had leaked the whole plan.[26] The Kaiser was no Bismarck, a silly, preening bully with no interest in the finesse of diplomacy. Internal tensions within the Empire between Teuton and Magyar were nearly at boiling point. Aehrenthal was steadfast in resisting Conrad's call for pre-emptive strikes against both Italy and Serbia at a time when these might actually have worked.

He sought at a summit with Edward VII and Foreign Secretary Charles Hardinge to maintain cordial relations with England whilst stressing Austria's ties with Germany. This was optimism indeed at a time when Britain was increasingly alarmed at the rise of the Kaiser's mighty navy.[27] Aehrenthal's efforts to placate Serbia were strewn along a very rocky path. Austria had frequently tried to bully her Balkan neighbour into an increasing dependency, much of this focused around the intriguingly named 'Pig Wars'.[28]

In 1908 he blundered, announcing rather blandly that he intended, with the quiescent consent of the Turks, to construct a railway across the Sanjak of Novibazar. On the one hand this was nothing startling but it did worry the Serbs. Izvolsky in St Petersburg, no great fanatic for pan-Slavism, couldn't get all that excited. The international press however did. The popular outrage placed Berlin behind the idea, (wrongly, the Kaiser had no interest in the project). Izvolsky was forced to backtrack and make threatening noises. He made capital from the fury of the Serbs by promoting the concept of an alternative railway line from Belgrade to the Adriatic, not a proposal Austria would wish to entertain. Aehrenthal had seemingly grabbed space for Austria at the heart of European politics and diplomacy but at some cost and general opinion saw him as little more than Berlin's stooge.

Despite the furore, both ministers had separate priorities and were not (yet) at each other's throats. The Russian was dusting off the old question of control of the Dardanelles. This might have enabled the Black Sea fleet to intervene in 1905 and avoided disaster at the hands of the Japanese. The Austrian wanted to get his hands fully on Bosnia-Herzegovina to build up an imperial balcony to counter the uncertain pull of Serbia.[29] The dispute of the railway proposal was soon set aside and both men met in September 1908 at Buchlau, Aehrenthal's country house.

Neither man kept or certainly never published any notes but on 6 October Franz Joseph offhandedly announced the formal annexation of Bosnia-Herzegovina. An international outcry arose. Aehrenthal asserted that his opposite number had agreed to this in return for Austrian acquiescence in the Dardanelles question. This was stridently denied. Izvolsky seems to have misread the runes and his apparent or possible connivance reaped a whirlwind. Aehrenthal, who emerges as the cannier of the two, deftly riposted that he had not agreed to Russian ships passing south through the straits on a unilateral basis. All he was prepared to agree to was free passage for *all* naval vessels. The Russian huffed and puffed but was evidently outsmarted.

The opening of the Dardanelles was very much a personal project; public opinion in Russia wasn't interested; the navy had taken such a pounding its prospects were greatly dimmed. If it was a victory for Austria, it was a pyrrhic one. Had Aehrenthal been more willing to carefully nurture relations with Serbia, now broken beyond fixing, and played on their fears over Bulgaria, he could have defused the whole ticking bomb of pan-Slavism and secured the Empire's volatile Balkan frontier. Instead he chose to score points and look clever, another Bismarck, but those days were long gone.

The folly of politicians has always provided business for spies, the murkier the waters the greater the imperative for sound and manipulative use of intelligence. In a world of such duplicity, duplicitous men will always be the beneficiaries. The Aehrenthals and Izvolskys keep the Redls in work and provide platforms for still greater duplicity. Alfred Redl had always been a quick learner.

In Barry Unsworth's evocative *Pascali's Island*[30] the protagonist, Pascali, a lowly agent in the uncertain pay of the Sublime Porte on some nameless and largely overlooked Aegean island, sends in his regular reports to an unseen and vast bureaucratic labyrinth which remains as the surviving shadow of the once great empire. The state is all seeing but much goes unseen, every timbre and shade of human vice and weakness is understood and often ignored. In a world of such multi-layered shadows, Pascali plays out his role unnoticed, weak, duplicitous and sly. Only when he makes the mistake of becoming infatuated with an enigmatic Englishwoman do his emotions lead him into danger and for her, tragedy.

Something of this decadence had seeped into the Balkans in the years of Ottoman rule. This was so deeply embedded that independence and, in the case of Greece say, the savage wars which accompanied the struggle, could not erase it, the scars only becoming deeper with the overlays of local factionalism. The Austrians became heirs to the Turkish hegemony but could not escape being drawn into the mix. The fictional Pascali is no match for the real-life Alfred Redl but the two have much in common. They are not bad men, however evil is defined, merely the men of their times. History is the stage manager and they provide the drama. By the time he graduated, the young Alfred was set to rise. He wouldn't just fly, he would soar but, like Icarus, he would get too close to the sun.

Chapter 3

The Last Waltz

More frontier and less coherence than any other state in Europe [1]

It's generally and correctly said that the Austro-Hungarian Army of the Great War, and in the years leading up to it, represented the most diverse and complex military structure within the ring of great powers. Austria, for all her defeats, was still a great power, certainly the most enduring. The Empire and the Habsburgs had survived for six centuries, a remarkable achievement in itself.

Austria had absorbed many defeats, initially from those irritatingly competent Swiss. It had been hammered by Frederick the Great and again by Napoleon though cowed by neither. Von Moltke had disposed of Austrian power in a single *Götterdämmerung* at Königgrätz (Sadowa) on the Elbe in 1866. Yet the Empire, its Emperor and the mystique of past glories still clung like a tattered, shot-torn standard.

Besides, it was not always defeat. Field Marshal Count Radetzky, the hero of the nineteenth century, won glorious victories in 1848–9, even though Austrian armies were fought to a bloody stalemate by the French at Magenta and Solferino in 1859. But Sadowa changed everything and was a major factor in the establishment of the Dual Monarchy a year after. The direction of the Empire shifted inexorably eastwards, more a Balkan outlook than a Germanic one. The Slavic and Italian communities within were galvanised by a new surge of nationalism. The Empire remained a polyglot agglomeration of often antagonistic racial groups: Germans, Czechs, Poles, Ruthenians,

Slovenes, Italians, Magyars, Romanians, Slovaks, Croats, Serbs and Jews.

This multicultural stew of types seriously inhibited the creation of a unified 'national' army. Austria-Hungary could never develop the intensely patriotic fervour of France or Germany. Drill commands were given in a plethora of languages and whilst overall numbers might, on paper, be impressive there was a marked difference between those contingents who could be deemed reliable (*Kaisertreu*) and those who weren't. The imperial agenda was blurred and often hindered, even obscured, by a whole raft of nationalist and ethnic sub-agendas. In round terms, the 'German' element amounted to about 28 per cent of the total. Another 18 per cent were Magyars so might be almost as fully counted on, but 44 per cent were Slavs for whom 'pan-Slavism'[2] came far closer to top of their priorities.[3]

Alfred Redl became infamous as a spy, the very epitome of treachery. But our view of treason is coloured by the later twentieth century, the 'John Le Carré' version. His influential fiction, heavily influenced by the real-life Cambridge spies Philby, Burgess and Maclean, has come to exemplify the breed. These were Englishmen who betrayed England. Redl was an Austrian who betrayed Austria yet there is really no such single unifying type within the polyglot empire. We examine the definition of treason against the Empire in subsequent chapters but what is certain is that Redl was very much the outsider, the parvenu ingratiating himself in the rigidly hierarchical framework, a low-born cuckoo in the gilded nest.

His position was always on the horns of a lemma. Without means or the appearance of means he could not rise. He did not have means nor any legitimate route to acquiring either wealth or status. His homosexuality was another hinterland of deceit, being gay was as damaging as being poor, being both was catastrophic. He needed cash and secrets were the only merchandise he had to sell. The growth in armies and in espionage ensured there was a ready market. We will debate what overall damage Redl's betrayal caused to the Empire but the probable reality is that this was not very great, if any.

Our hero lived in the era of the new military constitution, laid down after the formation of the Dual Monarchy in 1867. The armed forces were divided into three largely autonomous elements. These comprised the kaiserliches und konigliches (k.u.k) gemeinsames Heer, or Imperial and Royal Common Army, together with k.u.k Kriegsmarine (the Navy). Behind this front line stood the militia or territorials, the k.u.k. Landwehr with an equivalent naval reserve, but these second liners existed only in the German-speaking regions. Amongst the Magyars, the 'Royal Hungarian Honved' served an identical purpose. Obviously, the second line primarily fulfilled a homeland defence role but, like UK territorial units, they could and would be moved up as necessity dictated.[4]

A whole hinterland of complexity was added by the administrative process. The main or Common Army was organised by the k.u.k. Kriegsministerium which had a naval department bolted on. The Landwehr had ministries in their respective capital cities, Vienna and Budapest. Both used only their own native tongues. In the event of war, all three main ministries were to come under the umbrella of an overarching body, the k.u.k. Wehrmacht. Despite the obvious risks and complexities, the system did manage to function during the Great War.[5]

The ageing Emperor was titular head of the whole of the armed forces. In his eighties as the shadows of war loomed, he was very much part of the nineteenth century. Despite his age, the venerable and deeply conservative Franz Joseph was more than just a figurehead. He represented those six centuries of tradition, a very long line of continuity which linked the notions and ideals of medieval chivalry to the development on an army that would and must fight a great industrial war. Such totemic symbols are important and no other figure within the outwardly ramshackle empire came anywhere close.

Archduke Franz Ferdinand, as his heir, had been given the job of Inspector General of the Armed Forces. Nearest in stature was the Chief of the Imperial General Staff. Since 1906, this key post was filled by the wonderfully Ruritanian sounding Franz Conrad von Hoetzendorf. Extremely bellicose by nature – so much so he lost his job in 1910 but got it back a year later – and outwardly brilliant, he was in many ways limited by his own preconceptions. His weakness was that, however aggressive Austria was towards its two most obvious enemies Serbia and Russia, Germany would be wary of too great a commitment in the east as the Kaiser would always fear the French most.

The German Schlieffen Plan called for a major knock-out blow against France in the west on the assumption that the Tsar's armies would mobilise far more slowly. This wasn't at all what Conrad wanted to hear. Germany's west-looking approach implied Austria could be doomed to fight a two-front war with only minimal support.[6] Conrad had worked up plans to fight against Russia and Serbia and, if necessary, Italy, even though the Italians were, at this stage, at least nominal allies.

Despite their Chief's aggressive instincts, the Austrians' planning lacked the finesse shown by their German cousins. They didn't run the detailed war-games which characterised the micro planning of the Kaiser's armies. Many of the self-evident lessons of early twentieth-century conflicts, such as the Second Boer War (1899–1902) and the Russo-Japanese War of 1905, simply weren't learnt. Conrad also had a tendency to overestimate both the numbers of troops he had available to him and their capacities. These failings would bear bitter and costly fruit in 1914. Austria just wasn't ready.

Because of the hybrid nature of the various national and ethnic components, the Empire could certainly boast of an eclectic and colourful array of uniforms. The Magyar horsemen had a long and swashbuckling tradition, as had the Poles, and all the various groupings had distinct 'form' where long histories of warfare were concerned. Each had developed a particular style and there was understandable reluctance to see this all subsumed beneath a drab utilitarian uniform.

It wasn't until the reforms of 1867 that the wearing of body armour was phased out. Despite losing its cuirassiers, the cavalry fought a determined rearguard action to avoid donning drab grey. They finally went into a defining industrial war still wearing blue tunics and red breeches, topped with distinctive, dashing and not very practical shakos and *czapkas*. The sole exceptions were the modern mounted units of signals and machine gunners who wore pike-grey and managed to look like a twentieth-century army.[7]

Gunners, on the other hand, were professionals. The Austrian artillery had achieved notable successes and had managed to partly salvage what remained of the day at Sadowa, at no small cost to themselves. A legendary hero of the wonderfully named 'Battery of the Dead', the Czech gunner Jaburek was supposed to have had his head torn clear off by a Prussian round but somehow kept on serving his gun, *A u kanónu stál a furt jen ládoval* – 'he stands by the cannon and goes on loading'. Such unearthly devotion to duty was to be the gunner's trait.[8]

Despite this fearsome reputation, the artillery component was generally weaker than in other major armies. Generally, infantry divisions were under-gunned (forty-six pieces as opposed to the norm of sixty in Germany and seventy-two in France).[9] Unlike their mounted brethren, the gunners proved to be fast learners and the excellent cannon produced by Skoda enabled the artillery to catch up rapidly once war was declared.

In 1914, the Empire was able to put six armies into the field. Four would finally deploy in Galicia to block the Russians, a further two in the Balkans. In all, a total of eighteen army corps would be mustered. An army corps was made up of several divisions, the core tactical unit in the Great War. A division contained a number of brigades. In the case of the Austrian army, this was normally two and each brigade was comprised of two regiments. Four battalions of infantry plus one rifle or *Jäger* battalion made up the standard regimental muster.

Nobody had really foreseen what was coming. It was unprecedented. Four years of terrible conflict would shatter six centuries of durability. The Empire was, if nothing else, a masterpiece of the survivor's craft, cobbled, stitched and seemingly incoherent yet the Habsburg dynasty had somehow welded all the component parts into a viable structure.

The Empire could never afford to ignore this rich goulash of, often competing, regional interests and their various assemblies continued to have their say. This was at the time when the germ of nationalism or statehood was beginning to emerge in Western Europe, fuelled as in the case of England, say, by a reformed church. Such a unified society was impossible in the east and the Habsburgs found themselves in the long bloody wars of the seventeenth century under attack from both sides: Turks in the east, Protestants in the west.

The ancient office of Holy Roman Emperor was finally swept away by Bonaparte in 1806 but the Habsburgs remained as Emperors of Austria and suffered no loss of territory. Yet their orientation was shifting increasingly eastwards. Vienna became the centre of European polities as the victors met to decide on how the maps were to be redrawn and how the spoils might be divided. Emperor Francis II (1792–1835) did rather well out of it, a rich haul in Italy, the two choice provinces of Lombardy and Venetia.[10]

Those tricky demons, nationalism and liberalism, wouldn't go away however and even the energetic Metternich with his enthusiasm for repression couldn't suppress the rising tide of history. The crucial years, nearly two decades, between 1848 and 1867, saw the very foundations of the Habsburg Monarchy begin to shake, but not yet to finally fall. For the Empire, 1848 wasn't a vintage year. No less than five convulsions shook the imperial throne, conflict within conflicts as national and liberal ideals collided violently. It was the nationalists who fared best or least badly, so the process of liberalising was for a period derailed if not vanquished.[11]

Emperor Ferdinand, who had ruled since 1835, abdicated in favour of his nephew Franz Joseph who would in turn reign for sixty-eight years and become so closely identified with the conservative image of the Empire. By the time he died in 1916, the grinding attrition of the Great War would have gone on for two years and there were few alive who could remember a time when he had not been Emperor.

Franz Joseph would win prizes for longevity if not for enlightenment. He was an absolutist by upbringing and inclination, not over-burdened with grey matter, and wedded, increasingly anachronistically, to a body of tradition on which the sun was slowly setting. He was, early on, very much under the influence of reactionary advisers such as Prince Schwarzenburg[12] and, after his death,

Alexander Bach.[13] Even the army, which had saved the day in 1848–9, went into decline. In 1859, Austrian forces were hammered by the French in Italy, a return to the old days of Bonaparte. This time it was Napoleon III who, in championing Piedmont, unleashed his armies and Austria was defeated in two narrow and immensely bloody encounters at Magenta and Solferino.[14]

This debacle spawned a constitutional and fiscal crisis and led to the creation of an outwardly more liberal legislature but, in trying to promote an ideal of 'national' unity, pleased neither nationalists nor liberals. The Magyars, in particular, weren't satisfied, vying as they were for full recognition. An even worse military disaster was to follow at Sadowa in 1866. Von Moltke unleashed a *blitzkrieg* and the outmoded Austrian forces were hopelessly defeated in a single, set-piece battle.

No longer could the Habsburgs in Vienna still claim to be the leading power in the Germanic world. Prussia had suddenly and convincingly come of age. The axis tilted firmly towards Berlin and Austria was relegated to poor-relation status. This shift would only widen as the nineteenth century progressed. The new Germany went on to humble the old Habsburg enemy France in 1870–1. Her armies became the measure of efficiency and her industry boomed sufficiently even to challenge British hegemony.

The military disaster weakened Austria internally. Prior to hostilities Franz Joseph had hoped Prussia might become an ally and launch a joint assault upon France to recover Lombardy, lost after the defeats of 1859. The Austrians, naively, misread the situation. Prussia and Bismarck were bent, single-mindedly, upon unification of Germany and Austria was merely an obstacle. The Treaty of Prague which ended the war of 1866 sealed the Empire's relegation. The Magyars, on the other hand, got what they wanted, a redefined federal structure. Both now existed in parity, though of course still ruled by the Emperor. This dualism attracted critics at the time and ever since, though it is hard to define quite what other system could have been made to work.

Franz Joseph had seen the Empire further humbled and now also stripped of Venetia, its sole remaining Italian province. Habsburg prestige had never sunk lower. Prussia was now identified as the main enemy. The Emperor and his advisers burned to avenge their humiliation. They could never achieve this without the clear support of the Magyars. Giving autonomy to Hungary was infinitely less painful than allowing Prussia to elbow the Empire aside and steal her cherished seat as head of the table.

Even if the concept was flawed, it seems to have represented the only workable solution and Franz Joseph was crowned King of Hungary in June 1867 in 'the most colourful spectacle ever witnessed in Budapest'.[15] The two states were an odd conglomeration, neither separate nor wholly federal. Separated by language, heritage and culture, they shared only the defence and foreign ministries and their associated overheads. Franz Joseph controlled appointments within these but they answered to parliamentary bodies or 'Delegations' from each legislature which met separately in their respective capitals and only dealt with each other in writing.[16]

This compromise, cobbled together as it may have been, did strengthen the Empire overall and go some way to repair the shock of the disasters of 1859 and 1866. The Magyars became partners rather than subjects. When new challenges arose in the Balkans and the Russian bear began to stir, the Hungarians were very much part of Austria, unlike Austria-Hungary's very significant disaffected minority, the Slavic peoples, who shared a native bond with Russia. After 1879, Germany was no longer an enemy; fear of the Franco-Russian axis drove the German states into accord. Austria would never regain her dominance but she bought half a century of continued survival.

The weakness lay in the fact that the compromise created or allowed an entrenchment of Magyar dominance in Hungary and German superiority in Austria. Both would more jealously guard their privileges to the detriment of minorities. The question of nationalism would loom large in European affairs in the latter part of the nineteenth century and become enshrined in the Treaty of Versailles of 1919, the political obituary of the Habsburg states. John Mason makes a point, relying on previous quotations, that any great power can endure one 'Ireland' – an ethnically different often hostile society within its wide borders – but that Austria-Hungary consisted of not one Ireland but many.[17]

Minorities within the Empire, largely deprived of or denied representation such as Czechs, Poles, Ruthenians,[18] Slovenes,[19] Slovaks, Romanians, Croats, Serbs and Italians all had long histories of independent culture and achievement. A joint German/Magyar dominance offered them nothing, in fact it offered rather less than before as the two ruling elites so jealously fortified their positions.

Perhaps oddly, the advent of the Dual Monarchy worked in the Poles' favour. Their votes were needed to sustain a majority in Vienna and so they were effectively brought in with a whole raft of concessions, virtual autonomy. A significant number of Polish politicians held high office, the tide of 'Germanisation' was brought to a close and Polish culture and education allowed to flourish. The two great universities of Krakow and Lemberg remained centres of Polish culture.[20]

Even within Galicia, the Poles were not an absolute majority. Two-fifths of the people were Ruthenian, themselves a majority in the eastern marches. The conservative ruling elite, drawn mainly from the Polish aristocracy, rather looked down on them, rather as the Magyars did on non-Magyars in Hungary. Nonetheless, despite the resurgence of Polish nationalism in Galicia, the Poles were by no means disaffected.[21]

Another influential minority was the Jewish community. A large proportion of Austrian Jewish citizens were located in Vienna itself, perhaps 9 per cent of the capital's population. Many were extremely cosmopolitan whilst others, often from Galicia, tended towards the Orthodox. Jewish people became very influential in business and professional circles, though they were never really accepted in society.[22] As Gustav Mahler lamented: 'I am a thrice homeless man: as a Bohemian amongst Austrians, as an Austrian among Germans and as a Jew among the peoples of the whole world'.[23]

In a sense something similar could be said of Redl, an Austrian, never a Pole, but still from a poor family. He was a homosexual, automatically an outcast. Being from poor stock without patronage he'd have to earn his place in the military hierarchy rather than have progression spoon-fed by accident of birth. This incoherence of Empire at its very heart discourages the outsider yet creates a platform of opportunity for the ruthlessly single-minded.

John Mason points out, quite rightly, that the politics of late Empire from 1867 to 1914 were significantly shaped by economics. This is always correct, political choices very often follow the money. A very considerable level of fiscal inequality amongst the parts of Empire helped to fuel the surge of nationalism. After 1871, Germany's rise as an industrial powerhouse was meteoric, Austria trailed behind, more akin to the slow-burn of the Russian economy. Even by the dawn of the twentieth century, Austria was primarily a pastoral society. Over half the workforce was working in the fields even as late as 1910 and a rather higher proportion next door in Hungary.[24]

It is uncertain if Alfred Redl saw any other career path than the army, probably not. It appears to form a natural choice as few others were open to him. He had neither property nor any association with the land. He had no access to capital or family business to build upon. His father was a state employee and Galicia, even if the Poles enjoyed autonomy, was a long way and a mountain chain distant from Vienna. For a clever and ambitious young man, the army offered the only real route to success. It was at the heart of imperial society, so woven into the fabric of crown and history as to be indivisible.

> During the last twenty years before 1914 the military class had lost much of its prestige; the officer generally was regarded as a species of slacker, a man who shirked real work and the military class had therefore withdrawn more and more from the civilian. It was only among the lower bourgeoisie that people could be found who would be impressed by the status of an officer.[25]

Clearly Redl, quite uncannily, could be seen as fitting this unflattering profile. but Countess Landi here tends towards the vituperative. For a young man of energy, wit and ambition, there just weren't that many alternatives.

Dualism did not necessarily make for smooth running. The compromise had been effective in bringing the Magyars on side in general terms but the overall polity of the Empire was very far from harmonious. Between 1867 and 1914, Austria had a score of prime ministers, Hungary a few less (Germany on the other hand, appointed only five chancellors during the period[26]). The Austrian cabinet was technically an independent executive arm not fully answerable to parliament, but the legislature could be remarkably obstructive if it demurred. There were some forty political parties, affiliated to half as many factions – still rather a lot and not geared for ease or efficiency.

Alfred grew up in an era of liberal predominance which endured for a dozen years after the advent of the Dual Monarchy. By liberals we mean German liberals with a pronounced pro German bias. They championed a unitary rather than a federalised system and took little heed of minority aspirations. They tended to be middle-class professionals who favoured administrative reform, improvements in education and were broadly anti-clerical. Their reforms mirrored those of Bismarck in Germany (another who waged virtual war on the Catholic Church in the south). Despite this outwardly progressive agenda, the liberals did not seek to widen the franchise even at a time when less than 6 per cent of the overall population could vote.[27]

All attempts to introduce a federalist, more inclusive programme were rebuffed by the liberals but the foundations of their supremacy were dramatically undermined by the banking crash of 1873. This produced a distinct reaction against laissez-faire capitalism and after they opposed the acquisition of Bosnia-Herzegovina five years later, their dominance swiftly unravelled. In the elections of that year, the conservatives gained far more votes and an 'iron-ring' enveloped the liberals. Their power and that of parliament declined. From 1879 to 1893, this iron ring ruled with support from Czech and Polish conservatives.[28]

The final years of the nineteenth century and the opening years of the next, a countdown to oblivion, were dominated by the nationalist question. The old warhorse Prince Windisch-grätz was brought back into the saddle as premier but his ministry only lasted two years. His was a rather shaky coalition of the factions which had undone his predecessor Taaffe. This fell at the first serious hurdle, itself a minor matter, a dispute over parallel language teaching at a school in southern Styria.[29]

His competent successor was the Pole, Count Badeni who was able to further extend the franchise, adding a fifth category or 'curia' to those now eligible to vote. This was pragmatic, prompted by the need to secure Czech support in parliament and counter the weight of the conservative bourgeois lobby. His attempts to establish the Czech language on an even footing with German provoked inevitable resentment amongst the latter. Dislike soon turned to anger and open brawling. Badeni's ministry went down in the fallout and the ideal of parliamentary government, based on equal representation and fairness, was lost. Commentators consider 1897 the death knell for the Habsburgs: 'the realm was doomed'.[30]

This may be overly dramatic but the crown had increasingly to rely upon the use of emergency decrees – 'Article 14' – to get legislation through. Badeni's stint was followed by faceless bureaucrats, part of a state apparatus rather than democratic process. Both Czechs and Germans continued to feud. Von Koerber, the next prime minister, tried hard but fell foul of nationalist rumblings, quitting in 1904. An unexpected champion of electoral reform was the Emperor himself. Franz Joseph was, by inclination, an absolutist but was canny enough to realise that by enfranchising the workers he might create a counterpoise to the bourgeois hegemony in parliament.

At the start of 1907, the measure introducing universal suffrage (males over 24 only) became law. On paper, this was a major step towards full parliamentary democracy, but in reality it failed to solve any of the existing problems. The imperial polity was now grid-locked. The vertical lines of nationalism were criss-crossed by the horizontal bars of social class with the rising influence of the Social Democrats and Christian Socialists.[31]

By the end of the first decade of the twentieth century, parliament was fractured into thirty factions. Laws could not be passed, the whole system worked against itself. The last premier before the curtain fell was Count Stürgkh. He was forced to rely increasingly on the arbitrary sledgehammer of Article 14. In March 1914 he used this as a weapon to adjourn parliament so the legislature never got to vote on the countdown to war. Austria-Hungary blundered into Armageddon without a democratic mandate.

In 1908, the ageing Emperor celebrated his three-score years on the throne. Born a year before Alfred Redl, the Archduke Franz Ferdinand was successor in waiting. Though obviously much younger, the heir designate was equally authoritarian in temperament and notably resentful of the levels of Hungarian influence in government circles. Even if Franz Ferdinand could not directly control affairs, his influence expanded as the Emperor aged, leading one critic to quip, 'we not only have two parliaments, we also have two emperors'.[32] Some observers felt that the Empire would break up on the death of Franz Joseph.[33] Nobody at the time quite appreciated the impact those two fatal shots in Sarajevo on 28 June 1914 would have or how the single murderous act of a teenage terrorist would finally bring six centuries of continuous rule to a bitter and very bloody end.

Alfred Redl would not live to witness the start of war. His life and military career, his time as a spy, were part of what now seems an inevitable slide into catastrophe. With the inestimable blessing of hindsight it seems that the era was one of gloom and despondency. Yet this final twilight of the once great empire witnessed a soaring epoch of dynamic art and culture. There was pessimism but Vienna was the hub of a vibrant and creative society, a brilliant Edwardian twilight where all those fissiparous strands, nationalism, liberalism/ conservatism, socialism, reaction and progress all rubbed shoulders. Perhaps the Empire had just been there for so long that nobody believed it could all end.

Chapter 4

The Game

It was not till the beginning of September that Ashenden, a writer by profession, who had been abroad at the outbreak of the war, managed to get back to England. He chanced soon after his arrival to go to a party and was there introduced to a middle-aged colonel whose name he did not catch. He had some talk with him. As he was about to leave, this officer came up to him and asked: 'I say, I wonder if you'd mind coming to see me. I'd rather like to have a chat with you. '

'Certainly,' said Ashenden, 'Whenever you like.'

'What about tomorrow at eleven?'

'All right'

(Somerset Maugham)

For treason is like a tree whose root is full of poison, and lyeth secret hid within the earth

(Lord Justice Edward Coke, speaking of the Gunpowder Plotters in 1606)

In the summer of 1964, one co-author went to see *Dr No*[1] at a dingy, run-down cinema in Byker, one of the then decaying Newcastle's more decayed suburbs. A less likely match for the intoxicating world of fast cars, very fast women and sub-tropical locations would have been very difficult to imagine. This was the first of the Bond films. Two dozen or so have followed and the brand remains as strong as ever. As a boy, the co-author devoured every book, Fleming's life was nearly as racy as his hero's – Jamaica was very exotic in 1964 and naming your house 'Goldeneye' has always had a particular ring.

In the 1980s it was the turn of TV with *Reilly, Ace of Spies*.[2] Sam

Neill created a rival for Bond with the real-life Sidney Reilly.[3] Alfred Redl was a contemporary of Reilly. He was, in his own way, just as serious a 'player'. The exact consequences of his treachery, in terms of the overall effect on Austro-Hungarian military fortunes in the opening stages of the Great War was probably less catastrophic than has been portrayed.

Fiction, beginning possibly with Maugham, elevated the spy to hero status. Fleming boosted this to superstar level, followed by the more realistic Le Carré and dozens of others. The patriotic spy who fights the cold and dirty war on behalf of his or her country is sharply differentiated from the internal spy, the traitor who sells the nation's secrets to an external enemy. Generally, writers of fiction are unwilling to ascribe higher motives to the turncoat who may, nonetheless, be motivated by other ideological loyalties. This is pretty emphatically not the case with Alfred Redl. He was neither an idealist nor an irredentist. In all likelihood he was never blackmailed over his sexuality, which was far less rare than then admitted. He just wanted the money. The circus he'd built up needed a constant injection of funds to maintain its facade.

Redl's story is classic spy territory: coded writing, dead letter drops, running and 'turning' agents, surveillance, interception and a dozen other practices of the 'Secret World'.[4] But what is the point of espionage? The late Sir John Keegan defined various key elements:

- Acquisition – intelligence has to be found. That which is worth finding out, i.e. of value to an opponent, almost by definition, will be hidden. Whatever is already in the public domain doesn't require clandestine means. In Redl's day this could be mainly be found out using 'human' intelligence, spies or agents, signals intelligence – the interception and deciphering of the enemy's communications – and visual intelligence, gathered by photographing sensitive plans or documents or using reconnaissance aircraft, just beginning to come of age.
- Delivery – it's not enough to gather data, they have to be transmitted. This is probably the riskiest stage for the agent on the ground, yet

success is driven by urgency. The information has to be current or it has no value.

- Acceptance – the source has to be believable. The agent can expect to be distrusted by all sides. His controllers or 'handlers' have to be able to believe the truth or credibility of the material he's sending. This whole murky world is defined by suspicion: the agent may be a plant, may have been 'turned' or might simply have got it wrong. Ideally, the data should be confirmed by several reliable sources.

- Interpretation – it is unlikely that any one agent can supply a complete picture. This is very rare and explains why Redl was so valuable a resource for the Russians. He was at the very heart of the Austrian effort, the creator of much of it, a counter-intelligence officer's dream, no guesswork required. History does provide us with examples of what happens when even good information is misread. In 1941, the Allies had cracked the German Enigma and were able to obtain a complete order of battle for the projected German invasion of Crete. This should have been enough but in fact the information was misinterpreted and a wholly false picture of Axis intentions was constructed to the extent it undermined the entire defence plan and contributed to defeat.

- Implementation – having got the intelligence, what do you then do with it? Senior officers tend to be wary of spies or 'spooks' and events often move too fast, develop a momentum of their own. Von Moltke, architect of Austria's downfall in 1866, pithily observed, 'no plan survives the first five minutes of encounter with the enemy'. John Keegan, equally trenchantly, applies this to intelligence gathering – 'no intelligence assessment, however solid its foundation, fully survives the test of action'.[5]

Military intelligence is as old as war. Understanding the enemy and his intentions, his strengths and weaknesses, what might be termed strategic intelligence, is vital when planning any campaign. The tactical plan might have to be fluid but an insight into the opposing forces' long-term capabilities is essential. The more tactical elements, ascertaining the enemy's immediate dispositions, troop numbers and logistics, often depend upon good scouting and reconnaissance, traditionally using light cavalry. In both cases, how you interpret what is pretty much bound to be an incomplete picture is core to success.

With the emergence of industrialised warfare in the nineteenth century, the need for effective inter-state espionage increased. This was the beginnings of total war where the whole economic capacity of the state would have to be directed towards fighting and winning a modern war. Prussia's rise was proof of this, as was the course of the American Civil War which demonstrated, had the European powers been paying full attention, that the days of the great decisive set-piece battle were over and the new warfare was a process of grinding and infinitely bloody attrition. President Lincoln had the Pinkertons[6] managing his military intelligence (not very well it had to be said), but it would be the North's industrial might rather than the brilliance of her generals, none of whom was really a match for Robert E Lee, which would crush the South.

The nineteenth century was a boom time for spies. The world's great empires lived in permanent suspicion of each other's ambitions. For much of the century Britain was preoccupied, to the point of paranoia, over Russian intentions towards India. The 'Jewel in the Crown' looked to be increasingly exposed as the Bear marched inexorably eastwards over the roof of the world. This was dubbed 'the Great Game' played out across a vast canvas. The entente of 1907 might have defused the tension but it reignited with a vengeance ten years later after the Revolution. All previous bets were off. British imperial angst prompted the disastrous intervention in Afghanistan in 1839–42 and led to the destruction, almost literally to the last man, of the entire Army of the Indus. As late as 1904, the Younghusband expedition to Lhasa was spurred by fear of Tsarist ambitions. Kipling brilliantly fictionalised the Great Game with *Kim*.

The Game had its bumbling elements, gentlemen amateurs posing as scientists or archaeologists, but even as early as 1844 the Indian administration had set up a cryptographic unit, which enjoyed some real successes against agents of the Tsar. As the practice of military and counter-intelligence spread, diplomacy became increasingly intertwined, with military attachés often acting as spy masters. During the Crimean War (1854–6), Britain established its wordily named Topographical and Statistical Department. Map-making was clearly a vital function, and the need for organisation was dramatically underscored by the significant lack of maps of the Crimea; the army invaded blind.

Even in the twentieth century, the recruitment of agents as Maugham describes it was, by modern standards, rather ad hoc. He writes with some authority as he was himself a spy. In the aftermath of the Russian Revolution, Sir Mansfield Cumming, the dynamic head, indeed creator and shaper, of British intelligence, was keen to use all means to thwart Lenin and the Bolsheviks. An early aim was to keep Kerensky's Provisional Government in power and in the war. The Allies could manage without the Tsar but not without his armies, battered as they were by early 1917. Cumming instructed his top man in the USA, William Wiseman, to brief his American counterparts and bring them on side.

Wiseman was pushing on an open door; communism would never find many friends across the Atlantic. Soon in funds, he had to decide on the best man for the tricky job of actually getting the cash, secretly of course, to Kerensky. He knew about Maugham, who'd done a good job earlier in Switzerland and who was then in the US. Despite being very ill (he had TB), Maugham was excited by the brief and agreed. The job would not be easy and potentially very dangerous. If his mission was discovered, the embarrassment to the western allies would be considerable. He'd be completely on his own – 'deniable' in modern speak.

Maugham had only one key question. He'd worked previously as an unpaid patriot but had found most of those he'd encountered were both more cynical and being better rewarded. So he asked Wiseman if, this time, he was to be a paid professional. His employers got the message and he was soon on the payroll.[7] Redl wasn't a gentleman amateur. He couldn't afford to be. He needed to be a professional to sustain the image of being a gentleman. He was a self-absorbed cynic rather than any form of idealist.

Techniques of espionage had hardly changed from preceding centuries, though one invention which would facilitate Redl was the development of the 'spy' camera. In the early days of photography, equipment was primitive, bulky and slow. You'd need long exposure times and a portable darkroom. A French camera, the Chambre Automatique De Bertsch which was less than 40 mm deep led the way. After the turn of the twentieth century, pocket-sized devices like the 'Expo Watch Camera' revolutionized the art of covert imaging. The manufacturers boasted that this, around twice the dimensions of a pocket watch, allowed you to take pictures without being observed.[8]

When the storm of 1848 broke across the Empire, it took the Austrian army largely unawares and, two years later, an attempt was made to remedy the deficiency when the Evidenzbureau was first organised. This was fairly rudimentary and, by Great Powers standards, understaffed. Its successes during the Austro-Sardinian and Prussian wars were modest in the extreme. Initially, the score or so of officers reported to the Foreign Ministry, though daily reports were submitted to the Chief of Staff and through his office directly to the Emperor. Hamstrung as it was part of the Foreign Ministry which was chronically underfunded, it would nonetheless be with the Bureau that Alfred Redl would make his mark. He would energise and revolutionise the art of counter-intelligence. His betrayal, lasting a decade before discovery, would be its darkest hour.

One of the most influential personalities in the Empire at the outset of Redl's career was Friedrich Beck who acted as Chief of the General Staff (CGS), between 1881 and 1906. Franz Joseph was amenable to delegation and Franz Ferdinand didn't have that much say (he seems to have exorcised his frustrations by waging war on all manner of game which he slew in prodigious numbers). Beck had rather more power or certainly influence than even Count Schlieffen in Germany.

He was officially subordinate to the War Minister but received his instructions direct from the Emperor with whom he was on very cordial terms, verging on friendship. Franz Joseph didn't have many friends. He took his rigid devotion to duty to the point of monasticism. Even the testy heir, ever mindful of his dignity, permitted the CGS to sit rather than stand in his august presence. His overall standing was such he was able to procure the resignation of a hostile minister in 1902.[9]

In Vienna the General Staff had the combined clout of the German General Staff (GGS) and War Ministry, a pretty potent combination. As CGS, Beck controlled all departments including the Evidenzbureau (6th Section), together with Operations (2nd) and Railways (7th).[10] The Bureau did liaise with its German counterpart and was generally well up on the various separatist and proto-terrorist groups active within the Empire but rather less clued-up on external threats. The CGS failed to discern either the Russian recovery after the 1905 debacle or the actual strength of the Serbs in 1914 who were far from the rabble of murderous bandits they were perceived as being.

The very fact the Bureau was as incomplete and vaguely amateur as it was gave Redl his cue. Here was the perfect stage for the consummate actor, a series of curtains behind which he could create layers of illusion. He could be visible yet almost invisible, still of the officer corps and caste yet part of another shadier world where explanations could easily be shelved or deflected on grounds of security. This was a platform where duplicity brought plaudits, where the shadows could both magnify and hide. The Evidenzbureau was everything Alfred Redl needed and he became the master manipulator. It was only the scale of his own needs that finally brought him down.

His character suited the clandestine world of the spy and he became thoroughly versed in its techniques, now generally known as 'tradecraft'. He used the dead drop or dead letter box to pass on the secrets he stole. Essentially this is a simple means of passing on information between the spy and his handler. Using a dead drop means the two do not need to meet, thus the risk of detection is greatly diminished. Post boxes are ideal, everyday and anonymous, the agent hides in the crowd and the mundane is his shield. Redl lived his whole life this way, the business of spying was just a further stage. Ironically, this was where he'd eventually be tripped up.

If Austria lagged behind say Britain and Germany in the creation of an effective intelligence network, this was to his advantage. In a more layered, knowing and complex community, he would have had more chance of being rumbled earlier. Even MI6, for decades the exemplar of brilliant intelligence, was badly caught out by the post-Second World War/Cold War scandal of the Cambridge spy ring: Philby, Burgess, Maclean, Blunt and possibly more who inflicted significant damage over a very long period. Even when fingers were pointed at Philby, colleagues leapt to his defence and, for a not inconsiderable period, he was given the benefit of the doubt. The group's final exposure and the depth of their treachery nearly ruined British Intelligence and damaged previous close harmony with the CIA.

In Beck's day, the CGS corresponded freely with his opposite number in Berlin and rather less freely with the one in Rome. In the event of war, he would almost certainly have become director of operations. As it was, he oversaw plans for mobilisation, railway transport and concentration – the very sinews of industrial war. Courtly and engaging, he advised the Emperor, who was of an age with him, on general military matters and the strategic elements of foreign policy. All key functions together with tactical doctrine, field and fixed defences, armaments and supply were under his capable hand. [11]

Much of Beck's success was due to his personal relationship with Franz Joseph. When the old warhorse finally stepped down at the age of 76 and was replaced by the volatile Conrad, things changed. Von Hoetzendorf was from a newer generation, less courtly and therefore less to an ageing Emperor's taste. He was in fact the heir's nominee. On paper the power of the GCS grew but in reality, his influence waned. In Germany, the reverse was becoming true – the younger Moltke was listened to more rather than less. In Vienna the War

Ministry began to recover lost ground and was empowered to act as a brake on the chief's bellicosity.[12]

Though the War Ministry was essentially a political office, it was invariably, as in Germany, occupied by a senior general, the more outward-looking public face of the armed forces. The minister had to get the annual defence budget through the tortuous maze of the dual polity. His job was to pull together a draft after detailed consultation with the CGS and his naval counterpart. This was vetted by both home governments, sent back for amendments as needed and then the finessed draft was laid before the Common Ministerial Council – the Gemeinsamer Ministerrat (GMR). This was comprised of the common ministers, both premiers and finance representatives, with the military men sometimes included.

The GMR was chaired by the Foreign Minister and was habitually parsimonious; rarely did the ministers award all that was asked for. Once the immediate bargaining was done the proposed budget was sent back to both national Delegations for discussion. Generally, if the GMR had signed off on the proposals, the Delegations were not expected to demur but the home parliaments then had the responsibility of raising the actual cash through their tax revenues.[13]

This wasn't all. The perennial and thorny question of manpower needs remained and this became more intractable as enmity between the home nations deepened after 1900. At the outset of the Dual Monarchy, the Army Act of 1868 introduced universal conscription with an annual quota of 95,000 recruits. These could expect to serve for three years under the colours, with a further seven as reservists. By 1882, the common army had opted for a territorial mobilization system, very akin to the German model. This, coupled with a programme of railway building to open up transit through the Carpathians, placed the Empire well ahead of the Russians in terms of mobilisation and concentration.[14]

Seven years later, the quota went up to 103,000 young men, where it stayed until 1912. Compared to the other European powers Austria-Hungary was last in terms of recruitment and conscription, with only

0.29 per cent of her various populations under arms at any one time. Russia could muster 0.35 per cent; Germany, as might be expected, rather more at 0.47 per cent and France, perhaps surprisingly, even more at 0.75 per cent. The French, with a smaller population, could field twice as many troops as the Empire.[15]

France did not have a Redl but she suffered a far more major and damaging espionage scandal – the Dreyfus Affair. This whole saga was brilliantly brought to life recently in Robert Harris's fictionalised account *An Officer and a Spy*.[16] *L'affaire Dreyfus* was played out over nearly a decade from 1894. Captain Alfred Dreyfus was a native of Alsace and also Jewish. Both counted against him. Jews were seen as untrustworthy and Dreyfus raised the spectre of rampant anti-Semitism.

A gunner, Dreyfus was convicted of treason, of having passed military secrets on to the Germans via their Paris embassy. Germans, in the wake of the war of 1870–1, were easily as unpopular as Jews and mistrusted; paranoia was rampant, surpassing even British fears over Russian ambitions. Dreyfus got life with the sentence to be served on French Guiana, the well-named 'Devil's island'. He was kept in terrible conditions reminiscent now of US captives at Guantanamo Bay, except he was the sole occupant, the whole redundant penal colony with all its filth, horror and suffering was kept going just for the degradation of Alfred Dreyfus. It had been hoped he'd do what was expected of him and save a whole lot of embarrassment by blowing his brains out.

One man who had doubts, the hero of the day, was George Picquart who was, in effect, Redl's opposite number. He pointed the finger at another officer, Ferdinand Esterhazy, undoubtedly the real villain, even though the actual intelligence being passed to Berlin was exceptionally low grade. Esterhazy's involvement was easily glossed over and yet further indictments heaped on Dreyfus. Picquart was sidelined in a heavy-handed manner with brutal contempt which could have easily broken a lesser man.

Unease began to spread and Dreyfus became a cause celebre – one that vehemently split the nation. Leading literary figures such as Emile

Zola took up the condemned man's case. In 1899 Dreyfus was granted a retrial, another farce, and he was loaded with another ten years. But the pro-Dreyfusards refused to give up and, in 1906, he was finally exonerated and reinstated, as was Picquart who rose to become Minister of War. Esterhazy was allowed to slip quietly away into the obscurity of exile in England. It is one of the ironies of Redl's career that his treachery continued undetected whilst the Dreyfus Affair continued to rage.

Redl would seemingly be guilty of treason under any legal definition. Yet perhaps within the hotchpotch of the Austro-Hungarian Empire treason had a more elastic provenance. Austrians conspired against Magyars and vice versa; Polish, Czech, Croat, Slavic and Italian minorities intrigued freely by themselves and in concert with foreign powers. Loyalty was not necessarily a fixed perspective. Conrad had proposed pre-emptive strikes against the Magyars, Italians and Serbs – at the time, nominal friends. In these circumstances many adjudged traitors considered themselves to be 'freedom-fighters' and could point fingers at their accusers.

After the murder of Franz Ferdinand, the assassin Gavrilo Princip with twenty-four others was put on trial, accused of treason rather than homicide. The penalty, needless to say, was death. The defendants' brilliant lawyer Rudolf Zistler argued that, as the annexation of Bosnia in 1908 had never been ratified in parliament, the purported takeover was unconstitutional and therefore void. You can't commit treason against the state if you are not a citizen. This was an excellent argument, not that the court was listening.[17]

It has been said that the Empire exhibited a 'generic landscape of treason' in the last decade of its survival[18] and naturally this deepened dramatically after war was declared and led to some draconian and merciless interpretations. Redl, of course, didn't live to see the war but we could ask whether the fact of his treachery, at the very heart of the military elite and undetected for so long, at least partly fuelled this pernicious spiral.

Treason is an ancient crime, traditionally abhorrent – often viewed as a form of moral degeneracy. At the trial of Sir Roger Casement for treason in 1916, treason, as a crime, was defined as 'the gravest known to the law ... almost too grave for expression'. The nature of the offence, as with Redl, was linked to the defendant's 'homosexual depravity'.[19] Being a traitor like being gay was a sign of moral weakness and degeneracy. The offence always carried the most severe penalties and those found guilty could expect little in the way of clemency.

The Austrian penal code dated from 1852, Hungary's from over a quarter of a century later. Section 58 of the earlier code covered treason *Hochverrat*, which was defined in three ways:

- any attack on the person of the sovereign (which oddly did not extend to other members of the imperial family);
- instigation of any form of violent regime change;
- causing danger to the external security of the state, fomenting civil war at home or working to detach a part of the imperial territory.[20]

This last sub-clause was much in use after 1914. Those who wanted to create independent states from within were legion and fear of and revulsion against their actions from the centre multiplied once the shells began to fly. If section 58 wasn't a sufficiently wide net, crimes involving espionage also came under section 67. This covered 'crimes against the war power of the state'. Spying clearly came within this but the provisions could be used as a kind of catch-all against anyone suspected of any form of collaboration.[21]

Redl would have undoubtedly fallen foul of section 67. Almost certainly he would have faced the death penalty. As an officer, he was expected not to embarrass the state any further with the squalor of a trial; easier and less inconvenient for everyone and it spared his family some of the humiliation. The officer, heir to centuries of chivalric tradition, was expected to at least do the 'decent' thing when he was caught out. In no small measure this was a safety valve for the army who could then shove the unpleasant realities under the thickest carpet going. That was the theory or at least the hope.

As war paranoia increased, the propensity for treasonable activity was linked to irredentist ideology. This was somewhat bizarre as the nationalist doesn't recognise he's a citizen of the larger imperial polity. This wouldn't exonerate Redl, then or now. Though he was born in Poland, he never showed any sympathy with Polish or Ruthenian separatism. For Redl, it was always the money.

Another contemporary case was that of Cesare Battisti – an Italian nationalist demonised by Austria as a vile traitor but subsequently eulogised by post-war Italian sentiment as a nationalist hero. Born under imperial dominion and a well-known opposition representative, he'd 'defected' to Italy in 1915 in the belief, undoubtedly sincere, that his countrymen belonged there. As for other notable separatists, such as Thomas Masaryk, a case under section 58, *Hochverrat*, was prepared.

Battisti had the misfortune to be captured in July 1916 in Italian uniform and was immediately arraigned before a drum-head court-martial. The verdict was never in doubt, and he was hanged barely two hours after sentencing. The abuse and humiliation which attended his death quickly backfired. In the court of public opinion he was quickly elevated to martyr status.[22] That was never going to happen in the case of Alfred Redl. His treason was made grubbier because his motives were entirely mercenary. His sexuality, like Battisti's alleged embezzlement, merely fuelled indignation – traitors were necessarily degenerate.

If Battisti's case was bad, many minorities suffered far worse and more wholesale discrimination. During 1914–18 possibly just under 2,000 people were executed as a result of court-martial decisions and some 60 per cent of these were civilians.[23] Many more were simply murdered without the sham of a trial. Serbs and Ruthenians fared particularly badly. It has been alleged that over 30,000 Ruthenes were murdered alongside 3,000 thousand Serbs.[24] If members of those groups decided to side with the enemy then it's hardly surprising.

Treason, therefore, in the convoluted landscape of the late Empire is a variable commodity. Had Redl been motivated by nationalist sentiment, in sympathy with Poles or Ruthenes, he might have been judged a martyr rather than just a traitor. On all of the evidence, however, it isn't possible to award the benefit of any doubt. Alfred just needed the cash and he wasn't interested in consequences. The nationalists, insofar as he ever thought of them, were strictly supporting artists. His drama had only one principal.

In spite of this 'landscape of treason' and the swelling clamour of irredentist movements within the patchwork of empire, not all was suspicion and gloom. Conrad, in the run-up to war, still saw the army as the glue which held the fabric of state and polity together, 'lacking all cohesive basis for a state, the army can only rely on the dynastic principle'.[25] Laurence Cole points out that the Habsburgs had, since the mid-seventeenth century, used the army as a furnace for welding the state. [26]

Militarism had remained as part of the warp and weft in the imperial polity ever since, even if it had not consistently been dominant. The defeats of 1859 and 1866, crushing as they had been, were not so catastrophic as to dissolve the bond. The idea of universal conscription and the rising meritocracy of industrial war forged new ties.[27] Even if Austria could only be seen as strong as part of a wider alliance, latterly with Germany, and lagged behind the other Great Powers in terms of manpower and hardware, she was still in the ring. And why not, the Empire had seen off German and Swedish Protestants, the Ottomans, Louis XIV, Bonaparte and had survived Bismarck. Nobody could contemplate the realities of 1914–18 till they erupted or foresee this would be the final curtain:

> Military culture in imperial Austria must be viewed on its own terms, and its orientation around the values of loyalty and honour had far-reaching implications within the complex process of interaction between state, civil society, and national communities.[28]

The career of Alfred Redl as an officer and spy must be viewed in this particular context. It wasn't just the state he betrayed but the army. As an officer, he was bound into the complex chivalric code of the elite. His perfidy didn't just damage or was perceived to have damaged the national interest; he had struck at the foundations of this totem of imperial hegemony and from within. Was this deliberate and intentional, was he a political subversive striving for a cause? Absolutely not, Redl was his own cause. The damage he did or might have done was incidental, collateral – or 'spillage' in the harsh argot of today.

Chapter 5

The Evidenzbureau
(Intelligence Bureau)

Now let the Empire's enemies draw near,
we look forward to giving them a warm reception:
so that never again will they dare
to venture forth from the barren wastes of the East.
The German sword for German lands
So let the power of the Empire be upheld!
(Wagner, *Lohengrin*)

In this country the military spirit is only rampant among the highest officers. The officers of lower rank have no dislike for their profession, but they do not take it as seriously as the Prussians.
(Countess Landi)

There are many who would say a courtroom is the perfect stage and lawyers all consummate actors. In the judicial drama, the expert witness is a significant player. He commands his audience: the advocates, knights of the joust and even the kingly figures on the bench must take heed. While he speaks, he holds everyone's attention. Put him in uniform and he stands out, a peacock among dandies. It's hard to imagine a more fitting platform for that most accomplished of actors, Alfred Redl. Immaculate in his tailored tunic, buttons gleaming, gloves dazzling white, contained, respectful yet resonant with authority, the embodiment of the clique within the elite. The master spy and arch-deceiver gives compelling evidence against those accused of espionage and treason. This has to be one of history's more telling ironies.

'The treason trial well into the twentieth century was the ultimate theatre for a public power struggle, where regimes would don a mask of legality in order to eliminate those identified as traitors.'[1] Though Austrian paranoia over treasonable or alleged treasonable activities reached its witch-hunting nadir after 1914, the witch-finder general of the pre-war era was the most subtle traitor of all.

> Austria-Hungary ... sat on the edge of two worlds, with treason still mainly signifying disloyalty to the Habsburg monarch and his empire. In contrast treason for the rest of the twentieth century was increasingly interpreted ideologically, as a question of allegiance to a political system.[2]

Redl's treason probably falls into the more traditional category, straightforward betrayal of the Empire. We can't let him off the hook on ideological grounds. He shows no sign of any allegiance other than the personal.

Had Redl survived and escaped detection until 1914, his powers and his role would have expanded exponentially. Emergency powers gave the army and thus the Bureau far more control over civilian affairs. Latent tensions were let loose like the dogs of war: cases of political crime in Vienna before 1914 ran at about 18 per cent of the total, but once hostilities commenced, this figure rocketed twelve-fold.[3] Even before Gavrilo Princip fired those fatal shots from his .32 calibre Browning Automatic in Sarajevo, the Empire had been using treason as a tool to combat the irredentists.

In 1909, when Redl was very much in full flow, one of the most notorious treason trials was staged in Zagreb. No fewer than fifty-three Serbs were accused of treason and thirty-one of them were subsequently convicted. 'The prosecutor's remit was to stigmatise a broad swathe of Croatia's Serbs and he twisted the evidence accordingly.'[4] An English observer described the whole biased farce as a gross travesty of justice and was astonished that the whole notion of high treason 'had not yet been consigned to the lumber room of medieval phrases'.[5] Whilst this theatre of oppression was being acted out, Alfred Redl was selling real secrets; the gamekeeper was still primarily a poacher.

While Alfred was with the Bureau it was based in the Ministry of War building near to the Hofburg itself. Its predecessor (now marked only by a plaque adjacent to Starbucks) was on the site of the ancient Babenburg Court – the dynasty who preceded the Habsburgs. The newer building by the architect Ludwig Bauman has not had a good press:

> If you started your tour of the Ringstrasse at the plain and elegant Postsparkasse by Otto Wagner, you should be ready to take a strong contrast: One of Vienna's ugliest, most pretentious and most ridiculous buildings, the former 'Imperial and Royal Ministry of War'. Built on the peak of European imperialism and nationalist arrogance, the building reflects the spirit in which the Ringstrae was revamped in the late 19th century – and in which Austria, if not all of Europe, was driven into World War I.[6]

The building's design and construction has as tortuous a history as Redl's own career. Originally a competition was held amongst military engineers to see who could come up with the best design. One which found favour but was finally consigned to oblivion on cost grounds would have been a vast phallic tower of fortress-like proportions, an overblown version of a medieval keep. What was actually chosen was

> a super-sized version of Baroque style with overblown ornaments. However, the successor to the throne, Archduke Franz Ferdinand, found the design too humble and ordered bigger and better gates and a double-headed eagle on top of the building that was so enormously big that another floor had to be added to the design in order to support the metal bird.[7]

Franz Ferdinand was not renowned for his good taste in architecture yet the whole baroque fantasy, its frenetic facade built to shore up the tottering might of crumbling empire was yet another theatre set. It perfectly suited Redl's personal style and put him squarely in the very heart of the still beating pulse of Empire. His office, by contrast was austere, even Spartan, all business not show. He was, after all, the consummate professional.

Redl, at the heart of the web, had two areas of responsibility. He headed up the Russian section. This was a vital component in the espionage network the Bureau provided. Reports, sent in by the Bureau chief Colonel Baron von Giesl,[8] went straight to the top. A select band of nine officers ran the department, covering six main spheres of interest: Russia, Balkans, Italy, Germany, France plus Britain/USA/Japan.[9]

The team pored over journals and reports sent in, around eighty publications a day, and looked at human intelligence provided by the military attachés in the respective capitals: Paris, Berlin, Bucharest, St Petersburg, Belgrade and the Sublime Porte. Their combined efforts provided the meat in the annual budgetary sandwich Beck had to negotiate through the various byzantine levels. The Bureau's findings also informed strategy, tactics and mobilisation plans. The Evidenzbureau was the eyes and ears of the Empire.

If this was promising, Alfred's second job was the juicier plum. He was also chief of the Operations Section. He was responsible for all the covert stuff. He controlled the recruitment, payment and deployment of agents in the field, either directly from the capital or via a network of intelligence stations, based in command centres across the patchwork of imperial outposts. Those running the other sections looked to him for specific data. His web of agents was the antennae of the Bureau.

There was more, he also controlled counter-intelligence. Whispers came in through his own agents, from army and police sources. He had carte blanche to probe wherever and investigate whomsoever. He would finger suspects for arrest and provide the necessary expert testimony at their trails. For a counter-spy, there couldn't possibly be a better vantage.

His predecessor, a Major Wissowski, seems to have been rather staid, well versed in tradecraft – codes and ciphers, invisible inks, hollowed out walking sticks and false top brushes, the standard tools of espionage – but otherwise less than fully proactive. Under such guidance the intelligence section hadn't sparkled and was generally held in poor esteem. Here was the golden chance. In a single bound Alfred could mightily impress his superiors.

As ever he was assiduous. He studied the dark arts of espionage, liaised with seasoned professionals in the security services, brushed up on the law. He ventured out into the field to the listening posts at his home town of Lemberg, Krakow, and Przemysl (destined to be the site of the longest siege of the Great War and a massive defeat for Austria). He toured Graz and Innsbruck where Italy was the enemy and Temesvar, Agram, Sarajevo and Zara on the fractious Balkan frontier. Relentlessly, he quizzed police, army and serving agents. He was proposing to galvanise the whole Austrian intelligence effort. His capacities for hard work, laser-sharp insight and rapid analysis had never served him better.

His conclusions required diplomatic presentation, though with Giesl, it transpired he was pushing on an open door. At the heart of Redl's critique was the failure of the Bureau to analyse the material it amassed. Officers were seconded on a wholly random basis without any real selection for aptitude. What Alfred was advocating was a much more integrated and dynamic service. The ineptitude of some handlers meant agents could run their own 'paper-mill' – simply sending in fictitious reports, knowing they'd be believed and get paid regardless.

His chief had to agree. The Bureau was under-funded and had plenty enemies within the administration. Their Foreign Office masters weren't keen; many in the army felt the whole show was a waste of time and, worse, contrary to the gentlemanly code of honour. Spying was a squalid and proletarian business, not for men of position to sully themselves with, best done in the shadows. The Emperor agreed; it just wasn't done to snoop on people.

Von Giesl was impressed, very. Alfred was reassigned to counter-intelligence, spared the more mundane chores of the Russian desk.

From now on he was the universal spider and the web would be wholly of his own making. Captain Redl had reason to look forward to the new century with real optimism. He had arrived. Soon the shock waves were spreading amongst the high command; things at the Bureau were changing. Not that any of the detail was leaking, as Redl had radically tightened security. Each of the sections now operated discretely. Visitors had to be cleared and logged. The duty officer had to ensure that all waste material was collected and burnt. He also had to check that doors, desks and safes were locked. Major Wissowski was relegated to a technical support role (where presumably he was happiest). A security airlock was created to guarantee privacy in the ops centre.

Redl also needed to overhaul handling procedures. Since its inception, the Bureau had divided agents into three core categories:

- Patriotic volunteers – *Vertrauensleute*
- Foreign mercenaries – *Konfidenten*
- Special operatives recruited for defined missions, paid or not – *Kundschafter*

Handlers were generally the resident attaché or consul. This was cumbersome, disjointed and expensive. The Bureau was reliant on and funding too many intermediaries. Besides, and critically, nobody was spying on the spies so resources were haemorrhaging for highly dubious material. Worse, agents could be turned or dummy networks set up by an enemy to infiltrate the system. Alfred changed all of that. He took back direct control and filtered existing operatives through his own diligence and police supervision. Anyone who was found to be or suspected of being compromised was sacked without appeal. The Bureau had just got modernised.

He worked hard, without respite, at least fifteen hours a day, often seven days a week, the very model of a zealot. Gradually, he came to control every agent in the field, their recruitment, vetting, training and deployment. Only he knew their identities, his colleagues knew them only by number. Redl was in charge, fully and completely and the plaudits flowed. These were deserved. At this stage in his career there was no hint of betrayal, no whiff of treason. That would come later. Alfred Redl is two people – the dedicated and ambitious officer with very considerable abilities and the ruthless, cynical traitor who used his talent and position to sell his country's secrets. Probably, he was able to keep these outwardly irreconcilable elements compartmented. He had plenty of practice, hiding his private life, his sexuality, in the drawer marked 'personal'.

There is a distinct correlation between how a modern expert, in this case, Barry Royden who was the Director of Counter-Intelligence for the CIA from 1999 to 2001, and with forty years' experience of the 'game', defines what makes a good recruiter and what we understand of Redl's character:

> First, I'd say what makes someone a good recruiter. That's the hardest part of the business. And it's not the skills that you might think. It's not that they have a forceful personality and dominating personality like they're able to convince you to do something. It's much more that you're a people person first of all. (...) And then you want to project a sense of discretion – that you're a discreet, professional, competent individual.

As for the ideal spy:

> What you're looking for is someone that has access to really difficult information to get; information that you can't get otherwise. Its leadership intentions, military capabilities, the spy service itself – what they're doing against us – we're looking for access first. Then we're looking for someone who would have a reason to be willing to cooperate with you. It can be that they're not very happy with their career.[10]

Or like Redl, they need the money.

In January 1901, Redl received instructions, via the War Ministry but originating with the Ministry of Justice, relating to the impending prosecution of an alleged spy, Alexander von Carina. This was a high-profile affair. The accused was in his late forties, a cavalry officer who had served with logistics. He became infatuated with a voluptuous widow Countess Mazzuchelli, apparently undeterred by the fact her previous partner had blown his brains out on account of her extravagance which had ruined him. She very quickly beggared Carina who soon found himself arraigned on charges of financial irregularities.

Having attempted and failed the same remedy as his predecessor, he suffered a breakdown and was quietly pensioned off. Having learnt nothing from his tribulations, he married the woman. She'd learnt nothing either and his indebtedness multiplied. Needing any source of income he answered an advertisement for a copy writer and was interviewed in Vienna by a prospective employer who went under the name Mueller. His next meeting was in Paris where he was introduced to the publisher, Heinrich Walter. He got the job and began writing articles on defence and military matters. He was praised and well paid. He kept writing, a whole wide-ranging series of features, all of which were pulled together from information in the public domain. After three years, however, he began to suspect he was being used for intelligence purposes and ceased writing.

Redl went to work. To make any chance of a successful prosecution stick, he had to establish three things: first, a true picture of the man's character; secondly, whether his military role could have allowed him access to sensitive information and, lastly, to form a professional judgement as to his likely guilt. As ever, Alfred was the model of thoroughness. His quarry was generally judged to have been a fine and gifted officer and his superior officer felt he lacked any close relationships with other officers that would have facilitated gaining secrets. The senior officer's second-in-command gave a very similar opinion. Redl persisted and found one officer who suggested that Carina had in fact been close to two fellow officers, Captains Bruckner and Schirnhofer, and that this intimacy might have afforded the chance to view or even copy restricted material. The trail then went dead, literally. Schirnhofer had died and Bruckner was mad, confined to an asylum.

On this evidence he had to conclude that von Carina *could* have been a spy. Far more subjective, was he in fact an enemy agent? First, he identified Mueller as the cover name of a Captain Henri Mareschal, known to be an intelligence officer, and von Carina had correspondence with another official in the French War Ministry. Alfred was even able to provide a detailed physical description of Mueller/Mareschal. Von Carina had attempted to throw out a smoke screen by saying he'd only worked for these alleged French publishers and the French military were not overly concerned with Austria. Of course, their Russian allies were very much concerned.

Maps found in the accused's apartment showed plans of border fortresses, including Krakow. Von Carina blustered that these were just general background but Alfred studied both the maps and the actual fortresses, visiting all three of them, Krakow, Halicz and Zalesczyki. He concluded that the plans were sketched from actual observation and drawn in such a way as to show all the main points of defence. This was espionage not journalism. His final report was a masterpiece of research and evaluation:

In that Walter and Mueller are doubtlessly foreign intelligence agents with whom Carina stood in prolonged contact, he was without any doubt active in foreign espionage service. From his several years' employment as well as the significant payments which he received from abroad, it can certainly be concluded that Carina must have engaged in the betrayal of military secrets. It is also certain that he stood in connection with informed persons for the purpose of espionage ... This, taken with his mental ability and significant military career, causes Carina to emerge as a dangerous spy who, through his activities, has doubtlessly injured the military interests of the state.

The cold logic of this conclusion is inescapable – Carina, driven by desperation had got in over his head. He may have chosen not to know but he should have realised he was being used and the money he was paid exceeded by far what he might realistically have otherwise expected. Dangerous romantic attachments can lead very easily down the road to perdition. A few years later and Alfred Redl could have testified to that.

On 7 January, 1902, Alexander von Carina stood in the dock. In appearance, he was every inch the cavalryman, a gentleman. He pleaded not guilty. Alfred Redl would be the prosecution's expert witness. His preliminary written summary was read out in court and easily withstood the defence's initial probes. Alfred, immaculate, impeccable, mannered and precise was perfect. He carefully answered technical questions as they were put. His performance on the stand was masterly. So completely had he mastered and teased out each nuance of the evidence, so meticulously had he built his case.

He was, after all, the expert. Though he'd only been in the job a short while, he could pronounce with absolute confidence as easy assurance on the mechanics of spying and how Carina's conduct slotted so neatly into the frame. The amounts he'd been paid and the telling fact his alleged editor had even advanced a loan clearly suggested a more sinister relationship where the spy's indebtedness bound him further into the conspiracy. This was on day two of the trial and by late afternoon, the jury delivered its verdict. Alexander von Carina was convicted of espionage and sentenced to four and a half years of hard labour. In the circumstances and given the trigger-happy justice dispensed so freely during the war, this was fairly lenient. The star of the show, as the papers commented, was Captain Alfred Redl. This was just a beginning.

In 1903 Redl handled a series of lower level Russian spy cases. With the inestimable benefit of hindsight we can see that these were minnows thrown to the sharks to enhance Redl's burgeoning reputation. Doctor Bronislaus Ossolinski, already discredited on account of civil offences, confessed to having stolen railway mobilisation tables. He got a year in gaol. The others, likewise, collected pretty nominal punishments. For Alfred to give evidence, however, he'd have to access the mobilisation plans. For every area of espionage these expendables were supposed to be spying in, he'd need to review all the data. They weren't passing secrets, he was. For the cost of a few stooges his handler was gaining priceless intelligence and promoting the traitor's rise, very simple and very clever. The new Bureau Chief, Colonel Eugen Hordliczka of the General Staff, insisted Alfred stay in his current post and not be moved on according to routine custom. Beck himself gave the nod. The Russians were no doubt obliged.

Alfred was everywhere. His new chief, the state police, prosecutors, fellow officers all flocked to the undisputed oracle. He was the man. He was frequently on the move, briefing his agents across the wide breadth of empire. He breathed new life into the moribund carcass of the Bureau. He made it work and he wrote the manuals – *Methods for the Recruitment and Supervision of Informants*.

Towards the end of July 1904, Alfred played the expert witness at the trials of a pair of Russian agents, Simon Lawrow and Bronislaus Dyrcz. These two were sacrificial goats his Russian handler had offered to develop his protégé's career. Both were pretty low grade. Lawrow, rather pathetically, had tried to assert he was a Russian officer, though he later denied it. In court, Redl was summoned to comment on the likelihood. His testimony was a masterpiece of demolition.

> During my stay in Russia I had frequent opportunity to learn to know Russian officers serving in various categories, but I never encountered one, militarily speaking, so unknowledgeable, uneducated and so slightly conscious of his position as is Lawrow, for if their social education is limited, their military knowledge – at once obvious to any officer – is not to be denied, an appearance absolutely lacking in Lawrow's case. Lawrow is no officer but he does possess the minimum knowledge necessary to be a non-commissioned officer.

In a succinct paragraph the defendant's status is both diminished and defined.

Proving the guilt of the spy in a court of law, even when he's been offered on a plate is never guaranteed. So much of the evidence is cumulative and circumstantial. The prosecution faltered and it was left to Alfred Redl, as an expert witness who effectively filled the attorney's shoes, to wield the scalpel and the axe together, to show by dint of his vast experience just what the role of the spy entails.

On the vital subject of transport – mobilisation being key to the army's state of readiness, he showed how the agent could deduce warlike intentions from simply examining the rail infrastructure on the ground:

> If in a small railroad station with light peacetime traffic he sees significant ramp installations and numerous auxiliary tracks, he knows that here large troop movements will occur, that here large amounts of supplies will be loaded or unloaded.

As Redl knew how the Russians operate (rather better than the court might guess), the spy's guilt can be inferred from his actions:

> He [Lawrow] knew exactly how to maintain contact with the officials of his land, he knew that he had to transmit the results of his work immediately. He never received money by mail but always through a middleman. In a word, he possessed a knowledge of these arrangements so exact as to be held only by a person employed in this work.

Lawrow got twelve months.

After Lawrow's demolition, Redl went to work on the accomplice Dyrcz. It was alleged he'd been spying on Krakow's defences. This was an area of particular sensitivity, the city and fortress formed the gateway to Galicia. Once an enemy was through,

> I must stress that Krakow is the barrier against an invasion of Vienna. The fortresses lie so close to the border that they can be bombarded from foreign territory. Thus the enemy can begin siege preparations before the outbreak of war so that Krakow

on the first day of hostilities would have to defend itself against an enemy attack. Indeed, the attack on Krakow is the act through which war could begin ...

Cicero couldn't have put it better.

Redl spoke for a full half hour, rounding off a virtuoso performance with a contemptuous summary:

When the defence argues that Dyrcz as a spy would have had the necessary funds at his disposal while we have heard that he had to support himself in dishonest ways then I must reply that the foreign power in question rewards such spies only after they have delivered something, and indeed pay for the delivered information only after they have proved its importance and accuracy.

Only after Redl's unmasking would the full irony of this testimony strike home. Meanwhile, Dyrcz was sentenced to eighteen months.

Colonel Hordliczka was fulsome in his praise. Alfred Redl showed every admirable and desirable characteristic of an officer and gentleman. He was ripe for promotion, a view endorsed by the Deputy Chief of the General Staff, General Oskar Potiorek. Alfred devoted himself assiduously to his profession. He worked long and hard. His treachery need not negate his very real abilities and his boundless capacity for mastering detail.

His star continued to rise and he moved up a grade to major. He had barely scraped through the qualifying exam, but his track record catapulted him to almost the head of the queue. Redl was in a class of his own in counter-espionage. His techniques and reforms were his own and the four memoranda he bequeathed his successors formed a very sound platform.

Redl, whose whole life was artifice, understood the world of shadows. He had radically overhauled the Bureau, dragging his office from a largely disregarded outpost into the very heart of policy and command.

The Imperial Hofburg Palace in Vienna (Michaeler Wing), between 1890 and 1900.

Emperor Franz Joseph I, c.1880.

Habsburg Castle, Topographia Helvetiae, Matthäus Merian, 1642.

Lemberg around 1900.

"SAVE ME FROM MY FRIENDS!"

'Great Game cartoon from 1878' by Sir John Tenniel (1820-1914), *Punch Magazine*, 30 November, 1878. Political cartoon depicting the Afghan Emir Sher Ali with his "friends" the Russian Bear and British Lion. Text: "Save me from my friends."

Alois Lexa von Aehrenthal.

Guy Percy Wyndham and his brother George.

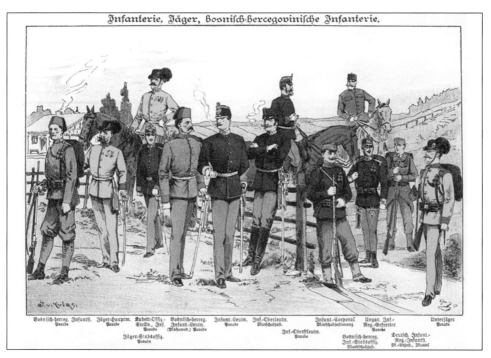

K.u.k. Infantry, Galicia, 1898.

Galician Infantry Regiment, Lemberg, 1884. Alfred Redl is listed under 'Cadets'

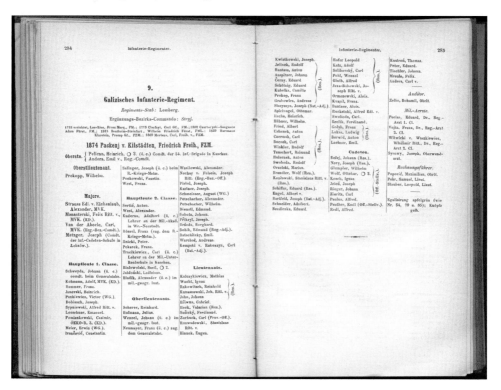

Neue Kriegsgefahr auf dem Balkan.

Zusammenstoß zwischen bulgarischen und serbischen Truppen am Flusse Zletowo.

Threat of war in the Balkans.

The seal of the Evidenzbureau.

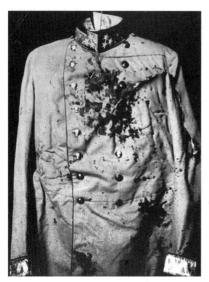

The bloodstained uniform of Archduke Franz Ferdinand of Austria.

Cover of the 'Petit Journal', 20 January 1895 (illustration by Lionel Royer and Fortuné Méaulle)

Austrian War Ministry Building, Am Hof (demolished in 1913)

Military Directory from 1905, Alfred Redl is now listed as 'general staff / Evidenzbureau'

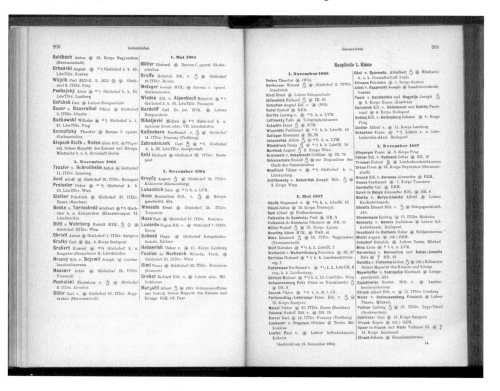

Kaiser Wilhelm II and Philipp, Prince of Eulenburg, 1890.

Roth, Joseph, Radetzkymarsch, 1st edition, Berlin 1932. (Foto H-P. Haack)

Franz Conrad von Hötzendorf in 1915.

Oscar Wilde's Trial, 'Police News', 4 May 1895.

Egon Erwin Kisch, GDR stamp 1985.

'Photo-Notebook' camera by
Rudolph Krügener, 1888. (Musée des
Arts et Métiers)

Alfred Redl and Baron von Giesl in an open carriage in
Prague. (ÖNB)

Marianna (May) Török de
Szendrő.

A 20-crown banknote of
the Dual Monarchy

Vienna Central Cemetery (Find A Grave). Nothing survives of Alfred Redl. His remains are buried under the wooden boards (these were used for a different burial).

Klaus Maria Brandauer as Colonel Redl in István Szabó's 1985 film.

A Patriot for Me at the Scala Theatre in Vienna 2015. Photo: Bettina Frenzel

Postcard of the Hotel Klomser, Vienna, c.1910. (ÖNB)

Chapter 6

The 'Ace of Spies'

Everything was peaceful. Vienna was sound asleep under the falling snow. The Emperor was asleep in the Hofburg and fifty million of his subjects were asleep in his lands. The son of the Officer of the Guards felt that this silence was also in part his responsibility, that he, too, was keeping watch over the sleep and safety of the Emperor and his fifty million subjects, even when he was doing no more than wearing his uniform with honour, going out in the evening, listening to waltzes, drinking French red wine, and saying to ladies and gentlemen exactly what they wished to hear from him. He felt that he obeyed a strict regime of laws, both written and unwritten, and that this obedience was also a duty which he fulfilled in the salons just as he fulfilled it in the barracks or on the drill ground. People had to be certain that everything was in its place.

(Sándor Márai, *Embers*)

'It has so far been established that Redl's espionage goes back to March 1912. It can therefore be assumed impossible that he started many years ago.' It is safe to say that hardly anybody believed Defence Minister's statement bore any resemblance to the truth. But is it now, more than 100 years later, any easier to establish when exactly Redl started his 'second' career? The answer is no. Existing sources are patchy. Archive materials got destroyed, and many top-secret events were never even written down. Then of course the picture gets blurred by countless adventurous assumptions, fictional adaptations and sheer disinformation.

There are, however, traces of believable information that lead, if not to final conclusions, at least to a clearer understanding of this spy master's games.[1] Amongst the countless statements from people who suddenly remembered that they had always had their suspicions about him and produced even more questionable stories, some remain that seem to bear at least hints of truth. Two of these occurred at high diplomatic levels.

In 1907 Count Lelio Spannocchi had taken on the post of military attaché in St Petersburg. In February 1909 he mentioned in a conversation with his British colleague, Lieutenant-Colonel Guy Wyndham, that he had been approached by a Russian officer who offered his espionage services. To his great surprise, Wyndham replied: 'Dear Spannocchi, no reason to get proud. I know of a high ranking Officer in the General Staff in Vienna who gives the Russians anything they want.' Wyndham refused to reveal details, which left Spannocchi rather worried. He decided to travel to Vienna and inform Colonel Hordliczka, then Head of the Evidenzbureau. At first he was not taken seriously and it was only when he showed his determination to get the War Ministry involved that Hordliczka agreed to take action. He delegated to case to the second in command, no other than Alfred Redl, who promised to do his best to solve the case, and asked Spannocchi to maintain silence.

One year later Spannocchi was accused of espionage himself. He was suspected of having received secret papers through the agent Count Eduard Ungern-Sternberg. Spannocchi tried to trivialise the affair, claiming he had never taken anything of importance, not even anything terribly secret. But nevertheless he had to go, and for the rest of his days he would blame Redl for this mishap, convinced that the Colonel had spun a sinister plan against him.

Around the same time, the military attaché in Chile informed his colleagues in Vienna about rumours he had heard from a Russian diplomat regarding Redl's respectability – no details have been preserved as to what precisely this term referred to. But whatever it was, it seems to have been considered serious enough to have reached Franz Joseph's aide-de-camp Baron von Margutti and possibly also

Adjutant General Count Eduard Paar, Franz Conrad von Hoetzendorf and once again Eugen Hordliczka. And this time, thanks to his veto, further investigations did not proceed, as he considered the accusations 'impossible'.

Another area where Redl came repeatedly under suspicion was his work as court expert. After his death the press pounced on just about every case he had ever been involved in, trying to establish connections between the accuser and the accused. Amongst the many cases there isn't one that led to clear conclusions, but some of them remain suspicious to this day. Redl had become something of a celebrity, a role that fitted him as naturally as his tailored uniform. Courtroom dramas have always been a good crowd-pleaser and his easy charm won him admirers in the press.

There is the case of Sigmund Hekajlo who had delivered secret military documents to the Russians. Two men were accused of having acted as accomplices: Major Ferdinand Ritter von Więckowski and Alexander Acht. Criticism arose from one of Redl's colleagues. Military counsel Hans Seeliger not only took a dislike to the way Redl used Więckowski's little daughter to find material hidden in her father's desk. To his great surprise the court expert changed his mind dramatically during the interrogations. Suddenly he seemed convinced of Więckowski's innocence. This also attracted the attention of Seeliger's superior who decided to have a quiet word with Eugen Hordliczka. And guess what – the Head of the Evidenzbureau saw no reason to interfere.

The writer and journalist Egon Erwin Kisch was convinced: the Russian wire-pullers had considered Więckowski important enough to give instructions to spare him from any harm: a rather unconvincing theory, given that Więckowski and Acht had only been informers for the main agent Hekajlo.

Seeliger's brother Emil mixed authentic material with press articles and his own imagination and presented the case in his booklet 'Colonel Redl – the Spy' in 1920. To him there was no doubt that Hekajlo had been the perfect scapegoat to hide his own dealings. Hekajlo already had a chequered past, he was an embezzler and had spied for the

Russians, like Redl himself, strictly for cash. Alfred could now strengthen his own career by presenting his superiors with incontrovertible evidence of Hekajlo's guilt.

Hans Seeliger, who also wrote the screenplay for the 1925 film *Colonel Redl*, recalled:

> From the extensive interrogation of the defendant which often lasted far into the night, I had my first opportunity of getting to know Redl as a military expert. He repeatedly interfered in the course of the enquiry, pumped the defendant as to all details of his treachery, and thereby displayed a knowledge of places and facts which astounded me, and which often was dumbfounding (...) Now the over-zealous effort of Redl to make the defendant confess that he had sold the deployment plans to Russia was striking to me. Hekailo spiritedly denied this when with an easy laugh he said, 'Captain, where in the world could I have obtained this deployment plan. Only someone in a General Staff Bureau in Vienna could have sold that to the Russians.'[2]

Historians Moritz and Leidinger found no evidence to support a connection between Redl and any of the three accused men.

The other case that attracted considerable interest over the years was that of Paul Bartmann who called himself the 'most dangerous of spies' and proudly claimed his espionage had cost Austria 40 million kronen. He had been convicted three times since 1895, accused of espionage for Russia.

Each time he was set free he resumed his former work, got caught again and encountered Alfred Redl as court expert. Oddly enough, it was the accused himself who, according to the *Neues Wiener Tagblatt*, expressed concerns about the man's character in a letter to his lawyer: 'Redl is ambitious, he has no backbone towards his superiors. But he's not finished yet. If he will be able to resist temptation, even if it's just half as big as big as the one I faced, we shall see!'

The Colonel's name turned up in connection with many other cases, but the evidence turned from weak to basically non-existent. There was the case of Anatolij Nikolaević Grimm, who sold the Russian mobilisation plans to the Austrians, which convinced War Minister Kuropatkin of the need to establish a new intelligence department. There is proof that Redl received secret documents from Grimm. But this doesn't automatically make him a spy.

Grimm's spy-handler had been military attaché Erwin Mueller. The Emperor was not amused. That his attaché should be exposed as a spy-handler was a disgrace, an affront to honour. Redl agreed but for more pragmatic reasons. *He* reasoned, correctly, that an attaché above suspicion could in fact learn far more. He'd be invited to military manoeuvres and gain automatic entree into upper levels of the host nation. Otherwise, he was bound to be under constant surveillance and excluded. Better by far to leave the attaché out of it and employ a series of resident agents, paid professionals who could stay in the shadows. This was wise and clever; moreover, the generous allowances paid to the diplomat could cover the costs of the agent. This would keep the 'suits' in accounts happy.

As a significant additional bonus, the agents were easier to control and Alfred would provide a series of templates for intelligence gathering which would ensure that only useful, relevant information was incoming. Performance would guarantee a much stronger case when it came to the annual horse-trading over funds. It was neat and thoroughly professional. It also made Redl perhaps the single most important officer in the imperial service. The actor was now impresario.

If spies hide in the shadows, spy-masters can sometimes bask in the limelight. As we mentioned, Redl had become something of a celebrity and, even though his successes were often the gift of his Russian handlers, Alfred was every bit as masterful as he seemed, his knowledge was real. His insight was genuine, only the performance was false. He easily outshone the prosecutor Viktor Pollak, yet the two men were to become close friends.

Everybody fell for his charms and his smartness. The new century had started promising for the ambitious man, now in his thirties. He was already Captain of the General Staff and had just spent a year in Russia to learn the language. He already spoke Polish and Ruthenian. Chief of Staff Franz Conrad von Hoetzendorf remembered:

> Foreign experience and language skills. Apart from those officers who were well off and used to travel independently, and those who travelled abroad as attaches or for reconnaissance sorties, the General Staff was unsophisticated.[3]

To speak all relevant languages was essential for the cohesion of the monarchy, and appropriate training measures became more and more important over the years. Under Hordliczka, language studies became obligatory, and after the candidate had passed his test he was given a scholarship to spend time abroad.

After a brief stop in Lemberg Redl found employment in the Evidenzbureau, the Danubian Monarchy's military intelligence service, as part of the 'Russian Section', where he spent most of his time analysing information about the Russian army. Soon after he was assigned to the counter-espionage department where he remained until 1905, when he became Major. After two years as Chief of Staff with the Vienna-based Territorial Infantry Division he was made Deputy Head of the bureau. He remained in this position until 1911. In 1909 he received the Cross for Military Merit.

'Qualification lists', or appraisals that were periodically compiled for officers, described him as 'intelligent, hard-working and modest', 'allowed to have high hopes for himself', a 'strong, male character' who was popular with his colleagues and cared for his subordinates, a positive influence on younger officers, 'always surrounding himself with decent company that corresponded with his fine way of thinking'. We do know, however, that in 1907 and 1909 Redl modified or possibly even wrote these reports himself. How much, if anything, of the quotations originated from his superiors will have to remain a mystery.

High-ranking officers were also objects of interest to the Russian military attachés who were expected to send regular reports to St Petersburg. In Redl's case this job went to Mitrofan Konstantinovič Marčenko (also Matschenko), the coordinating point for Russian espionage in Austria-Hungary between 1905 and 1910 and by some considered the one who had actually managed to sign up Redl; more about this later. Marčenko described the Major as clever, efficient and focused, but also considered him to be devious, two-faced and disingenuous, a cynic and philanderer with a weakness for 'amusements'.

After his death, many an 'old acquaintance' came forward with a story or two about his life and character. Hardly anything is verifiable, but the common denominator is that Redl's prodigality and his homosexuality were well known in military circles. So how did he get away with it for so long? It was a combination of the 'esprit de corps' that had led to exaggerated ideas of togetherness and loyalty. Chief of Staff Franz Conrad von Hoetzendorf was seen as a flagship of this rigid and fake value system and was heavily criticised for failing to recognise this dangerous villain amongst his subordinates. He indirectly defended his situation in his memoirs where he regrets having had to spend fourteen years on active service (*Truppendienst*) which made it impossible for him to get to know every aspiring General Staff officer.

Next, of course, Redl's position made people think twice whether or not to talk loudly about what they knew. Redl had power, and it looks like he had no scruples about using it against inconvenient acquaintances. Even after his death some of those who decided to send written evidence about the Colonel's love life to the Evidenzbureau, other military departments or to the press decided to remain anonymous. Now we hear about alleged lovers such as a lawyer named Heinrich Mittler, or a Lieutenant Oskar Feigl. An interesting portrayal of his character comes from a 'childhood friend':

It was no secret in our regiment that Redl, who was commander of the 12th company, had debts, but he won the sympathy of his superiors, especially that of the battalion commander, by writing all tactical tasks, war games and training exercises for him. At the same, time Redl's company was described as being very 'gschlampert' (messy). The magazine was always untidy, and his successor had a difficult job. Redl showed a particular weakness for his batman who managed to become a sergeant despite the fact that he had been an illiterate farmer. One had suspicions but remained quiet as Redl had made a number of friends for himself who basked in the halo of the future member of the General Staff. He and his clique enjoyed the full trust of the Colonel, while other officers were oppressed.[4]

May we safely assume that the author of these lines was himself one of the 'oppressed'? Another officer, Poldi Schmidl, added the picture of a sadist who enjoyed imposing harsh penalties for minor offences. Last but not least for many contemporaries, a betrayal of such proportions by a member of the General Staff remained simply unimaginable. To August Urbański he remained the helpful, cheerful companion, above any suspicion of whatever kind.

Even decades later Theodor Körner, social democrat and later Austrian President, would not deny that he had considered Redl a friend, which led to accusations of a homosexual relationship between the two army commanders. He even admitted that he had considered him a genius with regards to his intellectual capacity.

We often met for morning coffee in the cafe near the *Telegraph Bureau*. Like everyone else who knew him, I liked Alfred very much. He was always dignified – entirely the gentleman – but in a very friendly way. I think he liked me because I held a number of radical ideas for the reformation of the Army which we used to discuss. I personally enjoyed our association because he was a brilliant man to talk to. He knew a great deal about military and international affairs but more than that, his knowledge of human behaviour was startling.[5]

In the run-up to Redl's endgame dozens of spies were caught, the press fuelled ideas of networks and spy rings, with Redl pulling the strings. So far no convincing connections have surfaced. Instead we find the sad stories of countless small criminals who desperately tried to make a living for themselves and contacted the Russian intelligence service on their own accord. Despite delivering material of rarely any importance for very small remuneration, they faced up to more than four years in prison.

So let's return to the bigger players. We have already mentioned Marčenko, the Russian military attaché. He was a colourful character. August Urbański, now Chief of the Evidenzbureau, described him as unpleasantly nosy. The heir to the throne Franz Ferdinand found pleasure in the company of the diplomat who appeared to be keen on a harmonious relationship between the two powers. But the tide turned against him. One of his informers, Alfred Kretschmar (or Kretschmayr) von Kienbusch, was exposed. He told the story of his grudge against the system after not having made the career he'd thought a man with his qualifications deserved, and earning only a small salary. He offered to provide information about the k.u.k. artillery for a modest maximum sum of 50 kronen per assignment.

This was a lie. Kretschmar von Kienbusch had received monthly payments of 200 kronen. It also turned out that he had already worked for the three previous Russian military attachés. He described himself as a kind of 'inventory' that got passed on from one to the next. He had also served the needs of Italian and French clients, and in more than twenty years he had accumulated in excess of 30,000 kronen. He was sentenced to nine years and four months. Marčenko and his wife (nicknamed 'Vera Violetta') left Vienna after Franz Joseph ignored the couple at the court ball, as the newspapers reported. He had in fact also been encouraged to go on vacation.

Marčenko successfully pursued his career back home until the 1917 Revolution put a halt to it. The Kretschmar case had cost the constantly financially struggling k.u.k. intelligence service 8,000 kronen, and also made them even more aware of their information deficit regarding the

Russian army. Its origins go back to the year 1903 when the two powers had moved closer together. Unfortunately for Austria-Hungary, the Russians had different ideas of mutual trust and cheerfully continued to spy big style on their old foe.

The Danubian monarchy's Evidenzbureau under Hordliczka, with its limited resources, had its main focus on the Balkans, for good reasons. They were also obsessed with the thought of an Italian invasion in the case of Franz Joseph's death. Russia was just a minor worry. Maximilian Ronge, Redl's successor as Head of the Kundschaftsbureau, the Evidenzbureau's counter-espionage department, recognised the vulnerability and kept his eyes on the case. But he failed to see that the biggest enemy sat in their own midst, in the person of his own boss, as Redl had advanced to Deputy Head of the Evidenzbureau in 1907.

Marčenko's post was filled by Michail Ippolitovic Zankevic. According to Ronge, the new military attaché, who had already worked in Vienna between 1903 and 1905, knew he was being shadowed, but seemingly couldn't care less. What did he have to lose? It was the informers who took the risks, not the diplomats. Zankevic, who believed in the inevitability of a decisive battle between Teutons and Slavs, operated a whole network of spies, including the brothers Cedomil and Alexander Jandrić. This was another case that made headlines, just one month before Redl's death. The military authorities tried to handle the affair internally, even asked the Hungarian President to control the press, but failed. It later turned out that one or two employees of the War Ministry had boosted their salaries by passing on information to journalists.

One of the reasons why the case was so explosive was Cedomil's friendship with the Chief of the General Staff himself. They had attended the same military school, and some suggested they had been very close, and that Jandrić got access to sensitive material through his friend's advocacy.

The driving force however seems to have been Alexander, who copied and passed on whatever his brother unearthed. Their Russian purchasers were particularly interested in the documents that showed the redeployment of k.u.k. troops during the Balkan Wars. Alexander would later admit that he had forged countless documents. For each of these he was paid several thousand kronen. Zankevic played a crucial role in the affair. He was the middleman, and he didn't even try to hide his connection to the brothers from Croatia. Alexander even visited him at home. In the end, Alexander, the civilian, went to prison for five years. His brother had to face nineteen years behind bars. Zankevic went on holiday.

The proximity in time to Redl's case seemed to indicate a connection. But the military authorities could not find any evidence that he was one of Zankevic's agents, nor that he'd had any involvement with the two brothers. Several decades later it turned out that they did have something in common after all: when Cedomil Jandrić was arrested, Max Ronge handed over his Browning to the officer on duty, in case the arrested put up resistance. Jandrić behaved and the pistol went back to Ronge's office in the War Ministry. Only a few weeks later it had its next appearance. But this time the weapon was used.

Another major player was Nikolaj Stepanović Batjušin, the notorious boss of the Razvedka in Warsaw.[6] After the Second World War a writer called Arthur Schuetz aka Tristan Busch, a strange character with an eventful life history, published his version of the Redl story. Schuetz had himself worked for the Austrian Hungarian intelligence service, which led many others, including Asprey, to believe that he talked facts.

It was he who came up with the story that Redl was blackmailed because of his homosexuality by a Baltic German named Pratt and forced to spy for the Russians. He then went on to describe the Colonel as a child of evil who made deals with Batjušin over champagne and caviar, and sent his fellow Austrian spies to their doom. There are indicators that he had indeed passed on names to the Russians. Lists were found in his flat in Prague after his death, and Maximilian Ronge thought it likely that Redl had betrayed his compatriots in this manner.

However, historians Verena Moritz and Hannes Leidinger went to the Archive of Military History in Moscow in search for evidence and found none. Batjušin mentions Redl just randomly, mainly as an example that even the best agents make fatal mistakes. It seems that to Batjušin, Marčenko and Zankevic he was nothing more than an officer of a foreign power.

But there is one military attaché we haven't looked at yet: Vladimir Christoforovič Roop, based in Vienna 1900–5, another quirky character. In 1902 his name cropped up when the Italian Umberto Diminich sold him secret k.u.k. documents. Redl was on the case and Roop's involvement was swept under the carpet, for 'diplomatic reasons'.[7] Alexandr Samojlo, who at that time worked for the Russian Intelligence Service in Kiev, tells us in his memoirs how he bumped into his old friend Roop one day, probably in 1903. He offered to pass on to him his contacts in Vienna. Leidinger and Moritz suggest that Roop already knew that his days in the capital were numbered.

When Samoljo suggested travelling to Vienna to meet these people, Roop replied that his best contact, a certain 'R' who worked in the General Staff, would almost certainly refuse any direct engagement. In a 'spy list' compiled by Samoljo in 1913 he mentions 'No. 25', an agent who 'delivered highly secret and valuable information'. Due to a number of inconsistencies historians and writers, in the past, found it unlikely that 'R'/'No. 25' and Redl could have been one and the same man. But Leidinger and Moritz point out the crucial similarities: both '25' and Redl passed on their materials in photographic format. Most importantly: many documents Samoljo mentions in his 1913 report correspond exactly with the ones that were found in Redl's flat in Prague.[8]

It is quite possible that not even Roop knew the true identity of his best informer.

Maybe it really is a coincidence that this man who held this position of trust within the army became a criminal. But is it also a coincidence that nobody noticed it? Is it a coincidence that nobody became suspicious when this officer who descended from a family of small means lived the life of a grand seigneur for fourteen years, with his own automobile, and spent around 100,000 kronen every year?[9]

There is no doubt that people were aware, but Redl had power, and he knew how to use it. And this was Vienna. A city where, as Zweig asserts, 'one lived well and easily' if one had the means and ability to ignore the rising storm. In 1880, the city had had some 726,000 inhabitants; by 1910 the city had ballooned to the highest figure in its long history, 2,031,000.[10]

Under a calm, mirrored surface there was tension, trouble and uncertainty, major social and political problems. The old stability had begun to crumble. In the nineteenth century everybody had known where their place was. State, military, aristocracy, church, they held the power and determined everybody's life. At the turn of the century this system started to show cracks. A loss of orientation took over, and with it a sense of doubt of everything and everyone.

The novel *Radetzky March* by Joseph Roth (1894–1939) is probably the best fictional example of these personal conflicts. Its main protagonist is a man representing law and order, whose ideas about the world have been predefined by many generations and who is deprived of his security and authority by a sudden process of change.

Not far from the Habsburg palaces and villas an underbelly of poverty sprawled out across the city. Between Ringstrasse and the famous Wienerwald (Vienna Woods) lay whole districts of slums where occupants, if they were lucky, lived ten to a room. Many ended up sleeping in the labyrinthine sewers. When the journalist and satirist Karl Kraus (1874–1936) declared that 'the streets of Vienna were paved with culture unlike any other cities that made do with asphalt',[11] he was of course being sarcastic.

With this loss of orientation came a wave of craving for pleasure. Vice waited round the corner. Wannabe spies roamed the dark alleys just like the many prostitutes, trying to make a living; tormented souls of the kind Arthur Schnitzler portrays in his plays and novels.[12]

The nights were filled with all sorts of 'affairs of honour'; jealous brawls, illegal games, every imaginable petty crime. Foreign intelligence did not have to look too hard to find their informers and agents, far from it. Most of them offered their services on their own initiative, often referring to their harsh circumstances, sometimes even threatening to commit suicide should their pleadings not get heard.

In Redl's early days at the Evidenzbureau appraisals described his financial circumstances as sound, but not as wealthy. He seemed to have been one of the lucky ones. The army paid their officers only pitiful wages, and more often than not they found themselves in debt from a young age. But once again, the appearance was deceiving. Redl had already struggled with debt before the turn of the century. Back then it was the father of an alleged girlfriend, Emil von Naswetter, who helped him out, with bonds worth more than 4,000 kronen. The relationship soon cooled, there has been much speculation about the reasons, but one of them certainly was that Redl showed no intentions of repaying his debt. Even after Naswetter's death he still owed the family 2,500 kronen, and despite his widow repeatedly asking him to pay the money back, he never did.

When Chief of the Evidenzbureau August Urbański searched Redl's flat in Prague on 25 May 1913, he found 14,000 kronen in cash, roughly his annual salary including allowances. But he also found thousands of pounds worth of unpaid bills. In July the k.u.k. Financial Procurator's Office informed the corps commander in Prague that his assets totalled approximately 35,000 kronen, with liabilities of around 30,000 kronen. Monetary claims were made by the likes of tailors, dentists, jewellers and saddlers. This must have meant a huge disappointment to a number of people who had hoped to get their share of the inheritance. Everybody had assumed Redl was a rich man. He had led an extravagant lifestyle, owned a house and three horses. His car alone, a Daimler limousine, had cost almost 19,000 kronen.

Amongst the legacy hunters were some of Redl's past employees. A former chauffeur requested pieces of laundry. This might sound odd, but the Colonel had excellent taste in clothing, he only wore the finest quality garments, and he liked them in abundance. His wardrobes were stuffed with uniforms and the softest batiste shirts, ninety-five of them. He also owned sixty-two pairs of gloves.

The commission that recorded the inventory has left us small insights into Redl's private taste. He had lived in a three-bedroom flat with an adjoining tack-room. The predominant colour in the whole flat was red. Baroque walnut furniture stood in contrast with cheap pictures and knickknacks.[13] In December 1913 the whole lot went under the hammer, even a bundle of dirty laundry. The horses had already been auctioned off earlier in the year. The auction sparked huge public interest. Everything from expensive jewellery and watches to curiosities such as Russian tea or candies found new owners.

While newspaper articles reported a dramatic change in Redl's lifestyle during 1906, financial auditor Vorliček stated that 1907 was the year when it became obvious that he had found some lucrative sources of funds. He spent up to 2,000 kronen a month just on hiring cars. Between 1907 and 1912 he paid more than 150,000 kronen into his bank account. It can of course be assumed that there were vast amounts that never even made it to the bank. In 1912 there is a sudden stop to the payments. In October, at the same time as he starts his new post in Prague, the balance reached its lowest point with 3,000 kronen.

It is rather sad but true: for most k.u.k. spies, no matter how influential, money had been the main incentive to betray their country. In Elio Petrie's 1970 movie *Investigation of a Citizen above Suspicion*, the protagonist played by Gian Maria Volonte, an Italian police chief, kills his beautiful mistress for no apparent motive other than, as it seems, to prove he can get away with it. He becomes part of the investigation, creates a series of suspects, including the dead woman's homosexual husband. Then he ensures each is removed from the suspect list and the trail leads to him. But even when he confesses, he isn't believed – this can't be happening, he is literally above suspicion. This is Alfred Redl, the officer above suspicion, respected, lauded even revered, his guilt like that of the fictional policeman is too unthinkable.

It would strike so completely at the very foundations that the suggestion might verge on heresy.

This is the consummate actor at work. He isn't pretending, he lives the role. It's the only part he will ever play and the whole of his life is a rolling rehearsal.

Chapter 7

The Betrayal

It's all a strange history, and histories never end, but go on
living in their consequences.
(Henry James)

Mark Trachtenberg has rightly suggested that the great French
historian Elie Halevy summed up the origins of World War I
in the Rhodes Lectures delivered at Oxford in 1929 only 15
years after the outbreak of the war in 'a single but quite
remarkable paragraph.' Halevy wrote: 'But everyone knew,
who chose to know, that, whenever Austria declared war upon
Serbia, Pan-Slavist sentiment would become too strong for
any Russian government to resist its pressure. Everyone
knew, who chose to know, that whenever Russia gave so
much as a sign of declaring war upon Austria, Pan-German
feelings would compel the German government to enter the
lists in turn.'[1]

On the morning of 28 June 1914, Franz Ferdinand and his morganatic
wife the Duchess Sophie,[2] set off on what was to be their final public
engagement. The royal couple travelled by train from the agreeable
Ildiza Spa directly to Sarajevo. Governor Potiorek, with a gleaming
motorcade, was in attendance at the station. Due to an early confusion
the Archduke and Duchess were driven off in an open-topped Grief &
Stift 28/32 open tourer,[3] a rather stylish sports saloon but without any
close security. As it was a warm day the hood was down. It is hard to
imagine any modern head of state or VIP being permitted to motor in

such unguarded style. The police escort were in the wrong car; just the governor and Lieutenant Colonel von Harrach rode with the celebrity pair.

To avoid giving offence to any locals, the military presence was kept to a minimum, no troops on the streets merely three-score local coppers. Sarajevo is an old city, with many narrow and congested streets, an assassin's dream as the motorcade could not and indeed did not intend to move at speed. Three assassins, armed with a mix of firearms and bombs, were in waiting. Two lost their nerve but the third, Nedeljko Cabrinovic, did chuck his homemade grenade. So far Franz and Sophie were lucky. The device slithered off the folded hood of their car and then detonated under the next, trashing the vehicle, cratering the road and wounding nearly twenty onlookers.

The failed assassin attempted suicide by a hopeful mix of poison and drowning but was no more successful. The toxic capsule failed to take effect and, as he leapt into the river, he found the water was only 13 cm deep. He did get a good beating from the outraged crowd. Another three would-be killers including Gavrilo Princip also bungled the initiative test. But for the tubercular teenager, there would be another opportunity.

Franz Ferdinand, if unshaken was not unstirred, protesting at the civic reception that having bombs thrown at him was 'outrageous'. His own prepared address turned up still spattered with blood. It had been in the car behind. Sophie calmed him down sufficiently for him to thank the assembled citizenry for their joy in his survival. There was unfortunate irony in this.

What should the royals do next? Cautious counsel was for them to stay in the sanctuary of the town hall till troops could be brought in. Governor Potiorek vetoed this on the grounds that the soldiers wouldn't have time to get into their dress uniforms – 'Do you think Sarajevo is full of assassins?' He concluded. It seemed like a good idea to visit those who'd been injured in the city hospital, driving there in the same open car with Colonel Harrach now clinging on to the left-hand running board by way of a bodyguard.

More confusion followed, directions became mixed. Princip had taken up station outside Schiller's Deli by the Latin Bridge. In the mix-up, Potiorek ordered the car's driver Leopold Lojka, to stop, reverse and change tack. By random chance the vehicle halted virtually in front of Princip. This time, the young assassin passed the test. He closed to within a few feet and shot both Franz Ferdinand and his wife with his .380 pistol. The Archduke was hit in the throat and like his dying wife remained seated.[4] The car took off for the Governor's palace and medical aid. Harrach asserted that Franz Ferdinand, before losing consciousness, dismissed his wound muttering 'it is nothing'. As had often been the case, he was wrong.

Alfred Redl was dead way before those two fatal shots were fired but historians have argued ever since as to how his blatant treachery might have affected the outcome of the opening campaigns of the war that followed. Some, including Asprey, argue that the effect was catastrophic, causing enormous loss to the Empire and affecting the outcome of the war. Others are far from sure. In the wake of the murders and after the failure of diplomatic manoeuvres, Austria ordered partial mobilisation, this was Plan 'B', a limited campaign directed at Serbia, undertaken by a group of three armies totalling eight full corps.[5]

At this point the Empire's attention was focused primarily on Serbia. Full mobilisation, however, followed only three days after the declaration of war. Once it became clear that a far larger threat was looming from Russia, both the emphasis and strength had to be shipped across to support the right flank in Galicia. Having to reverse the original plan strained the available logistical support, especially the railway network. On 12 August the offensive against Serbia opened, the two armies left in theatre pushed over the river obstacle of the Drina but soon ran into stiff opposition and fell back to their jumping off points.[6]

In Galicia, a further two field armies were bolstered by German 8th Army whilst the 2nd Austrian Army took up the southern flank. On 22 August, Austrian forces attacked towards Lublin, winning the first round at Krasnik and then the second at Komarov, forcing the Russians into withdrawal. To the south, the revolving door swung the other way. Both the 3rd and the late arriving 2nd Army were pushed back. They were worsted at Zlotzow and reinforcements had to be drained from the victorious units to bolster their crumbling position. This handed the initiative back to Stavka (the Russian General Staff), which applied fresh pressure all along the line. A yawning gap opened up between the 1st and 4th Armies. The Russians swarmed into the void and so three imperial armies faced possible encirclement. It was time to fall back behind the River San, which left the vital fortress of Przemsyl under siege.

In September, Conrad planned a second crack at Serbia, though this made no more headway than the first. The Russians had now turned to face the Germans and were massively defeated in the great battle of the Masurian Lakes in early to mid-September. The Austrian line, bolstered by German 9th Army, managed to win back some ground and lifted the first Siege of Przemsyl. This success was short-lived and the fortress was soon encircled again. A last battle at Limanova-Lapanov, fought as winter closed in during early December, once again saw the Russians forced backwards.

There was more heavy fighting along the Balkan Front; the 5th and 6th Armies pushed forwards and almost surrounded Belgrade but a timely counter-offensive pushed the Austrians back behind the line of the River Save. Both sides were depleted and exhausted as winter closed in. By the end of the year, the honours were about even.[7] Nobody was winning even though Hindenburg had hammered the Russians, naming his victory as Tannenburg, revenge for the destruction of the Teutonic knights in 1411.

Was Alfred Redl to blame for this dismal lack of success? Most probably not – if anyone failed it was Conrad von Hoetzendorf. As commander-in-chief it was his muddled thinking that led to the swapping of available forces at the war's outset. In theory, this should have been workable, he had planned for it, but the task proved hard in practice and so weakened both fronts – with insufficient forces deployed against Serbia and the late arrival of 2nd Army in Galicia. These were strategic and tactical failures rather than intelligence-led. Von Moltke had observed that no plan, however carefully worked up, survives contact with reality and this is undoubtedly true. This is not to say that intelligence doesn't matter, it does.

Even at the war's outset the inherent instability of the Austrian military machine began to surface. Two primarily Czech regiments suffered heavily from desertion, large bodies of men going over to the Russians whilst the rest remained largely supine.[8] The Empire's failures arose from a dangerous mix of inadequate planning and internal, nationalist driven, tensions. On this basis it appears unlikely that Redl's activities had any direct bearing. Nonetheless, history shows that key intelligence delivered at the right moment can have a significant effect on outcomes.

Richard Sorge, Russia's mole in the German Embassy to Japan through 1941, gave some vital warnings on German and Japanese intentions which greatly assisted General Zhukov in the vital defence of Moscow. As early as 1265 during the Second Barons' War in England, intelligence on enemy dispositions, brought to Longshanks by an enterprising female agent, spurred a major spoiling raid which neutralised a whole wing of the opposition by a single, surgical stroke. The critical factor in both these instances was that the intelligence was fresh. Stale news is no news.

The 'Redl Case' was a cause celebre in 1913. For a brief moment on the eve of the World War, the people living in a time marked by disturbing events did not pay attention to the rivalries between the great powers, the fight over colonial territory, and the bitter struggles on the Balkans. In the midst of all the crises and the expectations of new and possibly even greater armed conflicts, the public briefly focused on the 'monstrous deeds' of a 'black sheep' that symbolized the monarchy's moral decay. Along with other scandals in civil administration and the army, Redl's betrayal contributed to the picture of a crumbling, moribund Danube Monarchy.[9]

The voluble fallout from Redl's unmasking and the botched cover-up probably says more about the state of the Austrian polity than it does about the longer term military and strategic consequences:

> This impression was further fuelled by other notorious espionage cases— such as the exposure of the spy network of the Russian military attaché in Vienna, Michail I. Zankevič, and especially the arrest of the spies Cedomil and Alexander Jandrić—and by a general 'spy mania' that characterized the period. Everybody expected a 'great matching of powers,' and strategists were obsessed with the idea of a preventive strike and a swift victory. As a result, there was great demand for information about the supposed enemies' military and political developments. More and more 'traitors' and 'enemy agents' were caught by 'counterespionage specialists'.[10]

If a state inclines to paranoia, then an affair like Redl will only deepen the fears. Years later, Ronge himself wrote that the total tally of 300 spy investigations in 1905 had seen a twenty-fold increase by 1913.[11] Galicia, Alfred's home province, was reckoned by intelligence observers to be 'infested' with Tsarist agents during that last, fragile year of peace.[12] Conrad's fear over Italian intentions struck deep and wasn't far off the mark. The Bureau had its eyes fixed firmly on Rome and the wave of border incidents that stoked irredentist activity. Von Hoetzendorf also kept a lookout towards Bucharest. Romanian inclinations proved fickle and their secret service – the Siguranta Generala Statului – hopped from one camp to the other. Outside of Berlin, Vienna had few reliable allies.

Even the tricky relationship with St Petersburg was far from consistent:

> In the course of trying to improve communications with St. Petersburg since 1900, the Evidenzbureau had reduced intelligence activities in Russia. The intelligence posts, which

in 1903 had a yearly budget of 20,000 koronas for their work 'in the East,' were cut to slightly over 6,000 koronas by 1906/7. The status of the Austrian espionage network had decreased; fewer and fewer informants were willing to continue in the light of these budget cuts. Not only did their numbers dwindle, but the remaining employees even cooperated occasionally with the Russian representatives, for example during the Russian-Japanese war of 1904/5.

The leaders of the Austrian army sanctioned further collaboration because they did not see the Russians, after their defeat in East Asia, as an immediate threat. Besides, the Austrians had already agreed to establish exchange programs with the Russians, and the future rivals in the 'espionage duel' on the eve of World War I learned the 'enemy's' language: The future head of the Razvedka post in Kiev, Michael Galkin, learned German in Upper Austria while Alfred Redl studied Russian in Kazan.[13]

Leidinger suggests that Redl's treason may have begun as nothing more sinister[14] than a friendly exchange between allies. Even if this is disingenuous, then the relaxed atmosphere would certainly have facilitated betrayal. The final unmasking and failed cover-up heightened suspicions and allowed the demonisation of Russian diplomatic personnel.

In December 1913 a 'Secret Handbook for Higher Commands' turned up in the public domain, and the Evidenzbureau wasn't at all sanguine about it. A man called Robert Langer had acquired one of Redl's Zeiss cameras with two film cassettes, at the auction of the dead man's possessions. When he didn't know how to handle his new toy, he asked a middle school pupil for advice, who then had quite a surprise when he developed the film. His teacher immediately contacted the military authorities. In the follow-up to this faux pas, every single person who had bought an item in the auction was located and their purchases checked. Those responsible for examining Redl's flat in Prague suffered a heavy backlash, most of all Urbański.

He explained that his main task had been close examination of the Colonel's desk – his orders had been to find out if Redl had given away mobilisation plans or other documents of similar importance. After seven hours he travelled back to Vienna with two suitcases and left the rest of the flat to Military Auditor Vorliček who stayed until the evening of 26 May, when he handed the job over to several corps officers. Between 25 and 26 May alone, 413 film rolls and 120 photographic copies of documents were secured. No doubt, Redl had been a busy spy. One of the officers later remembered having looked through about 1,000 postcards, in search for 'indecent' motives.

Urbański was now convinced that Redl had not only served the Russian Empire, but also the French and Italians. And he was equally sure Redl had not given away any recent material. How could he? He was stationed in Prague and no longer had access to all top secret documents. Here the Head of the Evidenzbureau was wrong. Even if Redl no longer had direct access himself, he knew plenty of people who did, especially younger subordinates would not dare to say no to a request made by the mighty Redl. After his death, several of them came forward, worried about their involvement and its consequences, and remembered how their superior had quite recently borrowed one or two current documents.

Having borrowed a document didn't necessarily mean passing it on to the enemy. Urbański gave instructions to watch out for marks left by paper clamps on pages that had been photographed, but even this was no final proof that there had been a buyer. Copies of documents of Redl quality cost the kind of money not even the Russians had spare. The official report concerning the documents found in Redl's flat was finished in July 1913. It stated that the papers that had been photographed included instructions for railway security, the mobilisation regulations for the event of war with 'R' (Russia) and 'I' (Italy) for 1912/13 and partly for 1913/14, the Ordre de Bataille 'B' (Balkan) for 1913/14 (apart from one page), as well as the Appendix for the Ordre de Bataille 1913/14 and a number of orders concerning Galicia. But, as the French military attaché Hallier put it: if the

Russians really had been able to gain access to the latest Ordre de Bataille and the rest of it, what were they waiting for, why didn't they just attack?[15]

Whilst the information Redl supplied on mobilisation plans, weapons, tactics, fortifications and planning was important, it constituted detail and confirmation. Most of the meat could have been gleaned, in broad outline, from careful analysis and agents on the ground. The nature of terrain, layout of roads and rail tracks, location of fortresses, supply points and arsenals could have been deduced by any military expert who knew the map he was looking at. The fear, suspicion and uncertainty which his treachery engendered were of equal value to Stavka of course – it's not all about how the intelligence benefits you, it's also about how its leaks confuse and disorientate the enemy.

Conrad for all his undoubted brilliance had major flaws. His first delusion was that his available forces were far stronger than they were. Had all his regiments been *kaisertreu* he might have been justified but they weren't and irredentist sentiment would come to weigh heavily – the cracks were showing as early as late autumn 1914. Just as bad, he viewed his enemies being far weaker than they were and less prepared. He had not effectively planned for a two-front war.

He undoubtedly hoped that he could launch a Schlieffen-type knock-out blow against Serbia before turning to face Russia. The confusion following an over-optimistic initial deployment weakened his chances fatally on both fronts. The two armies he threw against the Serbs simply weren't strong enough and his attempts to shore up the Galician Front foundered. Command and control systems and overall staff work in the Austrian armies just weren't up to the job. Conrad's planning would not just have to be as good as von Moltke's but even better to make up for the deficiencies in the make-up of his forces. Redl was a spy and a traitor but he didn't lose the war.

He did cause a very significant stir:

Several experts agreed that Redl's betrayal had 'indisputably' caused 'considerable damage.' Detailed evidence for this is hard to find—even though there are numerous records that document the increased efforts to put a stop to the game of potential enemy 'agents.' It was the scandals of 1913 that caused the Budapest state police to improve 'counter-intelligence measures.' While the border patrols in the eastern part of the Habsburg Empire were already participating in the proactive Kundschaftsdienst [espionage service]— 'K' for short.[16]

Ronge worked hard to plug the gaps and restore faith in the Bureau, a Sisyphean task. In May 1914, he hosted a conference on overhauling the whole business of counter-espionage. He was proposing much closer liaison between military and civil authorities and to create a new streamlined organisation, a central agency to 'exterminate enemy moles'.[17] He planned to make more use of the police in rooting out enemy agents, a more aggressive and proactive role. From an intelligence perspective this made excellent sense but the Vienna establishment demurred, perhaps this was a step too far. Yet the courts were in favour of tightening up the current laws and imposing much stricter sentencing.[18]

This wasn't just in response to Redl. The press and their 'indiscretions' were also a target. As was the Bureau itself which had been under attack since 1909 when its hegemony over espionage was challenged. In Germany, as ever the exemplar, responsibility was parcelled out between several General Staff departments and many officers felt Austria should conform. Ronge's own reforms were motivated partly by a need for self-preservation, keeping the Bureau in business.[19] His job was saved largely on account of the growing antagonism between Conrad and Franz Ferdinand which acted as a brake on any changes.

Some Russian sources, including the author M. Mil'stejn asserted that Redl had betrayed plans for a pre-emptive strike against Russia. Apparently the information was worth 50,000 kronen,[20] an enormous pay-off. August Urbański, former Head of the Bureau, confirmed much later, long after the war, that such information would be the lodestar of spying, pure gold. Even if this was the case, did it do the Russians any good? They planned no strike of their own and Conrad's vacillation in 1914 didn't suggest such a strike had ever been top of his agenda.

Austria had spies too, lots of them, and sources within Russia's high command. The Bureau had built up a comprehensive picture of Russian strength and capabilities, together with details of proposed mobilisation. How much weight the General Staff placed on this remains equally uncertain. Conrad seems to have remained focused on the deficiencies the war with Japan had highlighted and not to have taken too much notice of the reforms accomplished with the steady influx of French cash and supply. Even when Conrad was temporarily displaced by von Schemua in 1911/1912, there was a casual assumption of Austrian moral supremacy – the Russians being 'inferior on principle'.[21] This arrogance was dangerous in itself, writing the Russian army off as a just a horde of Mongol barbarians flew in the face of reason. In many ways their military machine was backward, under-equipped and indifferently led, but there were an awful lot of them.

> The opinions of the Austro-Hungarian army vacillated between over and underestimating the rival in the East. This also influenced the question as to whether the information acquired by the Evidenzbureau before 1908 was counterfeit or not. Nobody could accurately estimate the extent of Redl's betrayal. It seemed clear that he had handed over secret files that could have given the enemy at least an approximate picture of the Austro-Hungarian forces and military plans, which would have been difficult to compile from legally obtainable information and informants' reports. It was equally clear that Redl had dealt a significant blow to the Austrian secret service, the extent of which was hard to calculate. All efforts to hush up the 'monstrous affair' must be interpreted as attempts to control the damage.[22]

Conversely, unmasking Redl provided the opportunity to inflict a timely and cutting riposte to his Russian handlers and Mil'stejn provides no evidence that

> Redl handed over the Austro-Hungarian plans for a march on Russia. Apart from regulations concerning railroads and communications zones and from general information about the status of the Austro-Hungarian forces and a number of orders concerning Galicia, he had access to the mobilization regulations for the event of war with 'R' (Russia) and 'I' (Italy), as well as the complete 'Kriegs-Ordre de bataille' (order of battle) for the Balkans and the partial plan for 'R' and 'I'.[23]

Leidinger makes the point that such information, had it been transmitted, would have been of very high worth, given the importance of mobilisation and concentration of forces prior to any offensive. Equally, Redl was far from being the Russians' only source, though probably their best.

Assuming, for current purposes, that Redl did hand over all the mobilisation plans which came across his desk, this would have been a major blow to Austria. The potential enemy would have accurate and detailed knowledge. This material would be invaluable if the recipient power was planning an early offensive but there is no certainty this was the case. The Russian response in Galicia in 1914 was largely reactive and it's unclear how or indeed if Redl's filched plans assisted them.

> In the years before World War I, the central department of the Russian General Staff in St. Petersburg (GUGS for short) mostly sought to fill in some gaps in their knowledge. They claimed that the Habsburg army's 'battle order' was not complete yet, but that they were otherwise more than happy with the information they had. In fact, GUGS possessed 'most of the details concerning the mobilization of the Austro-

Hungarian army, in the form of photographed originals.' In May of 1913, shortly before Redl's exposure, the Russian army was well informed (as stated in writing) about 'the concentration of the Austro-Hungarian army' and individual 'k. u. k. corps' in the event of a 'war against Russia.' In addition, it was clear that the files Alfred Redl had delivered contained up-to-date information, a fact confirmed by the Russian intelligence officer Aleksandr A. Samojlo, one of the 'recipients' of the documents in question.

Consequently, the claim made by some experts that the main damage to the k. u. k. monarchy was done by Redl between 1907 and 1910 (thus before 1913) is incorrect. The most important documents clearly indicate the plans for the years 1913/14. The Russian files also indicate that Alfred Redl was seen as probably the most important but by far not the only 'top spy' in Razvedka's employ. GUGS noted that in the spring of 1913, they had been informed about 'the concentration of the Habsburg army' against the Russian empire by an 'agent operating covertly, a Czech citizen and former officer, who had worked on mobilization plans.' According to a note written the same year, the Russian military leadership had received 'war plans' that had been 'initiated by the Austro-Hungarian General Staff' but 'developed in Berlin'.[24]

It wasn't just Austria that proved porous, even the Germans weren't immune. Sergeant Gustav Wölkerling proved a very fruitful source, equally as valuable as Redl. Both traitors handed their material over to agents in neutral Switzerland. The Russian military attaché in Bern, Dmitrji Gurko, acted as collator and sent the data back to Moscow. Gurko also worked closely with his French counterpart Captain Paul Larguier.[25] It seems Gurko's convictions were entirely commercial and he was eventually rumbled and sidelined – not even the Italians would take him onto their payroll after that.[26]

After the discovery of incriminating evidence had forced the recall of the Russian military attaches in Vienna and Berlin in 1910/11, events followed each other in rapid succession after the turn of the year 1912/13. The k.u.k. Evidenzbureau informed their colleagues in the Hohenzollern army about an unknown man who temporarily lived in Vienna and who, among other things, offered mobilization orders for troops and fortifications in the German-Russian border regions for sale. The 'suspect' – it turned out to be Wölkerling – was finally arrested in February of 1913 after he had returned to Germany from a trip through Austria, France, and Switzerland. The cooperation between IIIb and the Evidenzbureau intensified and, after some k.u.k. officers had helped decode some secret documents, eventually led to the 'exposure of the traitor Alfred Redl.' The shock caused by his exposure and his death almost caused the entire Russian intelligence system to collapse, a fact of which the general public was largely unaware.[27]

Overall Russian planning was far from cohesive. One school of thought effectively ignored the Austrians, preferring to focus any offensive against East Prussia. It was felt the Germans would rest on the defensive in the west and attack *à outrance* in the east. This was the obvious aim of the Schlieffen Plan which called for a major knock-out blow in the west to clear France from the table before marching eastwards. France would always be 'the primary enemy':[28]

On March 9 of the same year, the British military attaché in Paris was absolutely sure that, if the Hohenzollern had to wage war on two fronts, they would first attack France, their 'primary enemy,' 'with all their might.' The Russian military leaders expected pretty much the same scenario at the time. Based on the information provided by their intelligence service, especially the 'war game' that had been developed in Berlin, they foresaw—months before Redl's exposure—the basic structure of the armed conflict at the beginning of World War I.[29]

Consequently, the French invested heavily in their ally's infrastructure, particularly the railways – all aimed at ensuring the Russians could get their armies into the field rapidly. Schlieffen had assumed, as a fundamental plank of his plan, that Russia would be the slower enemy to concentrate. From 1911, Russian Chief of Staff, Jakov G Zilinskji set to work on Plan 'A' – this overturned the previous notion that Russia would be attacked first. Consequently, and significantly, the process of concentration would be moved further west. This scuppered Austrian plans for an easy conquest of Kongress-Poland. 'The documents Redl had handed over, in particular, aided in planning and confirming Russian tactics.'[30]

Redl's leaks had not affected the overall strategic position in themselves. What he had done was to facilitate and enlighten Russian thinking now based on an accurate assessment of Austrian strengths, capabilities and intentions. This was clearly very significant. If the Austrians attacked they would be advancing against a far stronger enemy concentration than they'd envisaged. Yet Vienna appeared to be blind to current realities, a blindness that continued even after Redl was exposed. Urbański himself was one of those who had woken up and advocated a fresh perspective on war plans for Galicia:

> He thus advised the drawing-up of new plans based on a worst-case scenario. However, the operations office ignored his advice. In the meantime Urbański himself had stumbled upon the Redl affair . . . which ended his influence as an advisor.[31]

In February 1914, von Moltke gave Conrad a wake-up call. He warned emphatically that the rapid increases in Russian capacities could well signal the likelihood of a pre-emptive strike. This would kick off from further west than originally anticipated, focused on the Weichsel (Vistula) area, the broad river plain that bisects Poland. Conrad finally got the message, tailoring his own plans to conform far more closely to what was coming out of St Petersburg. He saw how exposed his forces east of Lemberg might now be in the face of a determined attack.

He restructured his whole plan to offer a flexible basis for both defence in depth and as a balcony for attack. He arranged his units in a steel ring, now shuffling more to the west:

> These changes, recommended by the officers of the Austro-Hungarian operations office as early as the winter of 1913/14, seemed to bother the Russians even sooner. As early as May 1913, after agents had reported a concentration of k.u.k. troops in the Cracow region, they wondered if the Austrians were redistributing their forces.[32]

This significant shift began to occur in the wake of Redl's exposure but we cannot be sure this was the reason. Far more likely it was the growing appreciation of the huge increase in Russian capability, prompted from Berlin.

Conrad still had to worry about the Romanians. They were perfectly placed to provide a shield for eastern Galicia and Bukovina but, as Austria had sided with their arch enemy Bulgaria during the Second Balkan, Crisis.[33] Bucharest began to have a rethink. The strategic situation was extremely fluid and if von Hoetzendorf had his blind spots, he was both capable and subtle:

> The k.u.k. Chief of Staff was more concerned with the danger of relying on a single crisis scenario. Since the correspondence with Moltke regarding the transfer of Russian troops to the west, he had been afraid of overlooking alternatives in other issues as well. He believed that it was not enough to anticipate different 'war scenarios.' Instead, the different variations had to be calibrated with each other and prepared in a way that would make them 'dovetail seamlessly with each other'.[34]

118

He was aware, as did in fact happen, that if the Russians struck whilst Austrian forces were heavily and closely engaged in the Balkans, then the whole Galician Front might crumble. His response was to have part of his available forces, the 'B' Squadron, ready to be switched between fronts. Initially supporting the fight against Serbia, these units could be rapidly redirected to Galicia. That was the theory but in practice the working out proved far from seamless.[35]

'It will all be over by Christmas' was a familiar refrain in the autumn of 1914. The generals just hadn't got it. Industrial wars are won largely by attrition not by swift and dazzling victories. There would be no 'Manoeuvre of Ulm' in the Balkans, Galicia or anywhere else. Austria was at a significant disadvantage compared to Russia. Put simply, there were many more potential recruits available to the Tsar. Improvements in supply, communications and logistics, while far from perfect, meant the Russians could concentrate their forces far more rapidly than before. Austria needed a quick win. Conrad was fighting time as well as enemies. Worse, his flexible strategy which seemed to work so well on paper did not fare at all well.

The autumn campaigning did not play out to Austria's advantage. At best all she achieved was stalemate on both fronts. In reality it was defeat. Was any of this down to Alfred Redl? Leidinger thinks so or at least maybe:

> If one looks at the individual events of the 'gambit campaigns,' one can easily see the connections with the scandal of May 1913. For example, as the Austrians were battling the Serbs, some units of the 8th corps, whose Chief of Staff the 'master spy' had been on his last assignment, showed signs of disintegration.[36]

He makes the point that the Russians would have shared some of their intelligence with the Serbs as close cooperation certainly took place.[37] This material was obviously going to be of great assistance to Belgrade. Nonetheless, we are not persuaded. What went wrong was bad planning rather than Serbian readiness. Conrad's strategic ideas just didn't work in practice so the force of concentration he needed never really arrived on either front. Had he been able to deliver a hammer blow against Serbia, then he might well have achieved an early decision. The failure then was his rather than Redl's. Clearly, the latter's treachery must have had some bearing but, in our judgement, this was very minor.

We certainly agree that Redl did not significantly influence events in Galicia.

> Even though it looks as if the war plans for 'R' had been heavily influenced by military intelligence, the 'sensational case of betrayal,' and the significant shortcomings of the Austro-Hungarian counter-espionage services, the calculations of the General Staff changed as a result of political and military considerations by the turn of the year 1913/14 at the latest.[38]

As we have noted, getting sight of military secrets is only part of the job of strategic analysis and much can be inferred from detailed study of the ground and data obtained from press and other general sources.

> Karl Bornemann, who would later serve as brigadier general in the Austrian army and who had met Alfred Redl when he was a young lieutenant, put it as follows: The Russians were well acquainted with 'established facts' such as the capacity of the railroads that connected the centre of the Austrian Empire with its borders, and they knew about the 'peacetime dislocation of the Austro-Hungarian forces.' On the other hand, says Bornemann, the k.u.k. General Staff had been revising instructions since the end of 1913, which included the transfer of troops to regions 'much further west.' Things did not happen the way the Austrians had wished because of their delayed 'readiness for operations' and because of the difficulties involved in 'directing' the 'supernumerary units' in Serbia to the 'north-eastern theatre of war.' Naturally, Redl's betrayal 'had no influence on this development of events'.[39]

THE BETRAYAL

In 1914, none of the generals, resplendent in the archaic extravagance of their Ruritanian uniforms, realised that they were the twilight shadows of a changing world. The war they embarked on destroyed the world they knew and which they thought, by fighting, they could preserve. Redl horrified them. That a member of this chivalric elite, the officer class, could betray them, could hold so sneeringly the values which had defined them for a thousand years, was unthinkable.

Chapter 8

Dolce Vita

Cafes are frequented for breakfast between 8 and 10 a.m., but chiefly in the afternoon and evening, when numerous Austrian, German, and other newspapers are provided. Small cups of black coffee, 'Nussschwarzer'; with milk, 'Capuziner'; larger cup or glass of coffee with cream, 'Melange'; cream, 'Obers Grosser Kaffee' means coffee and milk served separately.
(Baedeker, *Austria-Hungary*, 1911)

When Urbański entered the Colonel's flat in Prague it struck him as 'opulent' and 'feminine', nothing like a typical soldier's domicile. It was hard enough on him and Corps Commander Arthur Giesl von Gieslingen having to gather evidence against a trusted colleague and friend who was now believed to be a spy. They were still in a state of shock. But it would get worse. When Urbański opened the drawers to Redl's desk, he found several unfinished letters to a lieutenant based in Stockerau.

It slowly dawned on him that these were love letters. He also found perfumes and cosmetics, and a pile of 'disgusting' photographs that left no doubt about Redl's homosexual inclination. When he showed them to Hoetzendorf back in Vienna the Chief of the General Staff almost felt sick. The 'filthy' pictures showed Redl and a number of other men, amongst them the much younger lieutenant, completely naked. According to some papers they also posed in women's lingerie.

The young lieutenant in question was Stefan Horinka. He got arrested on the Wednesday, two days after letters and photographs had been discovered. To start with only his surname and initial had been published, which led the papers to accuse the wrong man. Then they asked the legitimate question why it had taken so long to arrest him. As this man had quite obviously been close to the master spy there was a good chance that he had known a secret or two, or even possessed incriminating evidence. And what exactly had been the nature of their relationship? The *Fremdenblatt* called it 'peculiar'.[1] The army still desperately tried to defuse and cover up as much as possible.

In the course of the scandal many claimed that everybody had known what had been going on. Others insisted that ordinary people who knew nothing of such aberrations had therefore been unable to spot them. Redl had on occasion been seen with women in public. This had led to wild rumours about countless affairs, with prostitutes, cabaret singers and aristocrats alike. The most popular version combined these stories with Russian femme fatale types who had dragged the poor helpless officer to his doom. Given that the man himself was a specialist in the field of hidden persuasion, the very thought of him losing his senses over the looks of a woman is rather absurd.

One of the accused turned out to be Marianna (May) Török de Szendrö, also known as Djavidan Hanum, a Hungarian noble born in the US, writer, painter and pianist, who had married the last Khedive of Egypt (he was also the last ruler of Egypt to have a harem). She'd later write a critical book on the subject, based on her own experience. When Redl met her in Vienna she and the Khedive had just separated. Neighbours heard 'knocking sounds' in her flat and found the regular visits by a Colonel of the General Staff suspicious. Worst of all, she suddenly left the city on 23 May. The knocking sounds later turned out to have been Djavidan hitting the keys of her piano.

Funnily enough a few years later she became associated with the Polish spy Jerzy Sosnowski who plied his trade in Germany. Marianna/Djadidan is a fascinating character and her richly faceted life still holds many mysteries. The authors feel that Redl might have been one of them. That she wasn't particularly precious about her methods is shown by a later incident, when, in Paris and desperate for money, she staged a hunger strike and feigned a 'collapse of malnutrition' in front of the flashing cameras. When the desired effects failed to emerge, she started picketing the British Embassy, to get her hands on a visa enabling her to travel to London to take a screen test for the film *Queen for a Day* produced by Alfred Golding [2].

It is of course possible that Redl was bisexual. Newspapers wrote about orgies and naked dancers he and his young lieutenant enjoyed watching. But it is more likely that he used women to entertain his male lovers and to cover up his own true inclinations. In the end, as far as we know, no evidence was found that suggested any kind of sexual or deeper emotional relationship to a woman.

His real love and passion belonged to men, especially to one of them: Stefan Horinka. According to the explicit testimony the latter gave at the Garrison Court after having been arrested for 'fornication against nature', Redl had approached him in 1908.[3] Under the pretext of wanting to check his health, the superior asked Horinka to open up his trousers, took out his penis and examined it for much longer than necessary. Similar occurrences happened, and over time Redl would also take photographs of the naked young man and of his penis in different stages of erection.

These photographs weren't the only ones the commission from Vienna discovered in his flat. There were pictures of the naked Colonel, and amongst the other playmates two of his former servants showed up: Andreas Nebel and Josef Schuler-Strasser. Nebel had worked for Redl for five years, between 1896 and 1901. But even after he had found himself a new job – with a little help from his former employer – at the Austrian-Hungarian Bank, he continued to live with Redl until 1904 when he got married.

Later on Redl kindly provided the couple with a useful present: their own house. Their benefactor became a regular visitor, and one of Nebel's own sons was named after him. In August 1912 he was put under police surveillance, when it became too obvious to his neighbourhood that he and his wife lived beyond their means. Both the police as well as the military investigations came to nothing but we think we should leave a big question mark beside this character.

Coincidentally, one of Nebel's bank colleagues was no other than Stefan Horinka's father, who asked him to request his big friend's intercession to get his son into the Infantry Cadet School. Josef Schuler-Strasser had been Nebel's successor, and again they seemed to enjoy more than just the ordinary master-servant relationship. Schuler-Strasser, who accompanied his employer on his final trip to Vienna, could be seen in public enjoying meals with his employer, dressed in fine clothes.

Both of them were lucky. The incriminating photographs turned out to be old enough to be statute-barred, and the court believed that they had been seduced to commit immoral acts against their will. Horinka also claimed in court, just like Nebel and Schuler-Strasser, that all the fondling had happened against his will, and explained the recent disagreement that had come to light through a series of letters with his refusal to have sexual intercourse. Luckily for him, one letter seemed to prove his statement and he too got off rather lightly, with three months in prison, although he also lost his military rank.

The letter dated 27 April 1913 does indeed leave us with an impression of Horinka having been put under pressure: 'You threaten to ruin me if I don't let you have your way. Fair enough, I'll rather perish than live the life of a strumpet who is forever worried that she might get thrown out.' As he couldn't see an end to it he announced his plan to leave the military, he was 'not prepared to be pressured'.[4]

This all sounds pretty innocent, but let's not forget that when these lines were put on paper, the two men had already known each other for almost ten years. Redl had made it possible for Horinka to start and to further his career, and the protégé had profited immensely from financial assistance over time. After Horinka had finished cadet school, his benefactor supported him first with 50 kronen (this rose to 100 and ended with 600 kronen) per month. In addition, he paid his rent, 1,000 kronen, not to mention the extra 12,000 kronen he spent on furnishing his flat.

They enjoyed holidays together, and expensive presents were a common occurrence, best of all: two horses and an automobile. Thanks to Redl he quickly climbed up the career ladder, from infantry to cavalry and on to the prestigious 7th (Franz Ferdinand) Uhlans. Horinka took full advantage of the fact that the older man was besotted with him. Even the most well-intentioned observer had to admit that this level of investment over such a long time was unlikely to be explainable by a couple of photographs and the occasional exposure of genitals.

Dark clouds appeared in the sky when Stefan Horinka fell in love with a young woman, Marie Dobias, his 'Mitzerl' (diminutive of Maria/Marie). She made the most of her lover's close relationship with his 'uncle'. Redl ended up paying for everything, rent, clothes, new teeth – and even abortions. Redl approved of the latter as he worried that the greedy girlfriend would try to force Stefan to marry her if she was expecting a child.

As we can see, no agents from foreign powers were needed to blackmail Redl. He had his hands full trying to keep his lovers submissive by financing their luxurious lifestyles. However, it is possible that some of these men threatened to give away his secret if their demands weren't met.

Gay male culture became visible in the Vienna of the fin-de-siècle. During the Industrial Revolution, large numbers of people moved into the city, many of them young single men. By the turn of the century, a number of guest houses, cafes and bars catered to a gay clientele, and baths and parks served as cruising venues for men to meet each other and have anonymous sex, a practice that seems to have gained popularity among gay men at this time.[5] Rent boys offered their services to 'elegant men of all ages' and often took advantage of their fear of being discovered.

And they had good reasons to keep a low profile. Homosexuality was illegal, and it remained so until 1971. In the eighteenth century, sodomy had been a criminal offence punishable by death. In 1768 Empress Maria Theresa had reformed the imperial law. Sodomites were to be beheaded; the body and the head were to be burned. Under

Napoleon sodomy was decriminalized in many European countries. In Austria, Emperor Francis II lessened the punishment from death to a prison term ranging from six months to a year – a considerable improvement. In 1852 punishment was again increased to a maximum of five years in prison. The term 'homosexuality' was introduced in the late nineteenth century by Karoly Maria Benkert, a German psychologist. At that point it was no longer a specific act that a person decided to commit, as in the medieval view. Sexuality was now usually seen as biologically driven; it appeared as an 'unchosen' characteristic of the individual. But when homosexuality is not chosen, it makes no sense to criminalise it. Instead, it was believed that people could be cured. Doctors and psychiatrists like Sigmund Freud, Richard von Krafft-Ebing or Magnus Hirschfeld campaigned for the repeal or reduction of criminal penalties. Public opinion was hugely influenced by the tragic end of Oscar Wilde after his imprisonment for gross indecency, and the suicide of Alfred Krupp.

The final trial of Oscar Wilde had left the public appalled and outraged at the 'crimes' that such a prominent man was able to commit. When the verdict was announced in the courtroom cries of joy and celebratory dancing commenced by the public in attendance.[6] The judge called the crime as so horrible that he had to restrain himself when he was forced to talk about it. He had presided over murder cases, but he felt that this one had been by far the most atrocious. He also echoed the public's fears that Wilde had corrupted younger men.

Wilde's health deteriorated in prison, where he had been condemned to hard labour. After his release he lived a meandering life, poor, ill and an alcoholic, until he died in Paris in 1900. On his sickbed he had proclaimed, 'I will never outlive this century, the English people would not stand for it.' He was wrong: almost overnight, a legend was born: Wilde the homosexual martyr and moral rebel. A young gay-rights movement embraced him as a hero of defiance.

Around the same time, German tycoon Friedrich Alfred Krupp enjoyed himself on the island of Capri, allegedly in the company of young men. Italy had legalised homosexuality in 1889 and had become an oasis for rich gay men from all over Europe. But Krupp wasn't just anybody – his family, arms and steel magnates, was (and still is) one of the most powerful in the country. He was active in politics and a close friend of the Kaiser. This made him a popular press target, and in 1902 the Social Democrats' newspaper *Vorwaerts* picked up the gossip and published it. He died soon after. It was assumed that he had committed suicide, convinced that he was doomed to a fate like Oscar Wilde's.

Unlike Wilde at the time of his death, Krupp had been popular with the people, and Kaiser Wilhelm himself went on a crusade against the Social Democrats. In a speech to Krupp's employees he praised his integrity and promised to 'hold the Kaiser's shield over the house and the memory of the deceased'.[7] This scandal was big news, not just in Germany but also in Austria and the rest of Europe.

Even more attention was given to another affair that concerned a close confident of the Kaiser – some say he was even more than that. This case became the biggest scandal around homosexuality in the German monarchy: the Harden-Eulenburg affair. Philipp, Prince of Eulenburg, was born into a noble Prussian family. In 1886 a school friend invited Eulenburg to his estate where he was introduced to the Crown Prince.

Wilhelm, twelve years younger than the 29-year-old Eulenburg, immediately fell under the spell of the charming, entertaining and cultured older man. When Wilhelm became Kaiser in 1888, Philipp, a member of the 'Liebenburg Circle' of aristocrats, the inner elite, became his closest adviser. He steadily encouraged Wilhelm to assume 'personal rule' (which he later regretted). Wilhelm's decision to sack Bismarck had been supported by Eulenburg.

In 1892, he was appointed ambassador to Austria-Hungary. Now and for the first time he was himself badly affected by the 'culture of intrigue' that dominated Prussia. He had fallen out with his former friend and ally Holstein, who contacted journalist Maximilian Harden to inform him that Eulenburg was a homosexual. He supposedly had relationships with the President of the Berlin City Police, Baron von

Richthofen, and Kuno von Moltke, head of the Berlin Military Garrison.

Harden's paper *Die Zukunft* had taken up the struggle against the Liebenberg Circle, which Harden regarded as the decisive obstacle to an extension of the spheres of influence of the German Empire. He forced Eulenburg to retire from his ambassadorship in Vienna. But when he continued to exert influence on political developments, Harden outed him. What followed was a series of courts-martial, five civil trials and accompanying libel trials. Ultimately, Eulenburg escaped further persecution because of his poor health.

Wilhelm II had been kept in the dark, but when he finally found out what was going on it didn't take him long to grasp that his own position was in danger. There had always been rumours about the homoerotic nature of his friendship with Eulenburg.[8] Now, his inner circle fell apart, homosexuals were named, and it would only be a matter of time until compromising details regarding the entertainment they had enjoyed together at Liebenburg Castle leaked to the public. The Kaiser withdrew from their friendship, Eulenburg was deeply hurt. He lived in retirement without further contact with German government or the Kaiser until his death in 1921.

It has often been said that the loss of Eulenburg's consensus-oriented influence on Wilhelm opened the way to the disaster that was soon to follow. High-profile cases like those of Krupp and Eulenburg furthered the rise of conspiracy theories and slowed down the progress public opinion had made towards homosexuality. Fears were stirred up. Gay circles were said to be conspiring everywhere, against the government, against the people, the 'homosexual intrigues' were a danger to the very foundations of empires.

These were the circumstances Alfred Redl had to deal with. Had he been a working-class man perhaps no one would have minded, but a high-ranking military official? No way! The *Danzer Armeezeitung* (Danzer Army Newspaper) wrote:

> … his love life was degenerated one speculated, one knew it. And this ill man was promoted to manage a Corps as Chief of

staff. A 'humane psychiatry' that accepts the inescapability of their sex life leaves the Urninge (homosexuals) to themselves in the darkness of their gatherings as long as they don't pose a danger to the public. But it is not a custom to appoint an Unmann (literally 'un-man') to a high military position, in the brightest light.[9]

Chapter 9

The Fall

Passports are not absolutely necessary in Austria-Hungary, but they are sometimes required in order to prove the traveller's identity, or to enable him to obtain delivery of registered letters.
(Baedeker, *Austria-Hungary*, 1911)

With the number of spies that were getting caught on the increase, Alfred Redl might have sensed that the noose was about to tighten. But he had other, personal troubles. And it looks like the reasons that led him to travel to Vienna and make a series of mistakes that led to his arrest had predominantly been of a private nature. Stefan Horinka, the man he was in love with, had threatened to leave him. Horinka did not reciprocate his feelings. He was engaged to a young woman. All Redl could do was what had worked on numerous occasions before: satisfy his greed for money and other earthly delights.

At the beginning of the year, the Evidenzbureau had received mail from their colleagues in Germany. They forwarded a letter they had intercepted. It was addressed to a Nikon Nizetas. The poste restante item had been held at a post office in Vienna. When nobody picked it up it got sent back to the place of posting, Eydtkunen, a small German border town. It had already been known as a stomping ground for spies to German intelligence, hence their interest in postal items. When they opened the letter, they found a substantial amount of money. Counter-intelligence boss Walter Nicolai decided to pass the case on to the Austrians.

Maximilian Ronge came up with the idea to take the – restored – letter back to the post office and wait for Mr Nizetas. Three detectives were stationed in the post office and waited to be notified by a ringing signal from the counter. Two more letters for Nizetas arrived, again carrying several thousand kronen each. The second letter had been posted in Berlin and contained a hand-written note by a J Dietrich, who hoped that his last letter had safely arrived and apologised for the delayed delivery. He assured Nizetas that his suggestions were acceptable, and asked him to send his reply to an Elise Kjernlie in Norway.[1]

Trying to give a halfway accurate attempt of Redl's last days isn't easy. Too many misrepresentations have clouded the sight, intentionally or not. Thankfully, Leidinger and Moritz have tried to separate the wheat from the chaff. In an interview forty years after the day when Nizetas finally turned up in Vienna's main post office, employee Betty Hanold remembered how she had immediately rung the bell and, despite being extremely nervous, tried to engage him in conversation until the three police officers finally made their appearance. They had a hard time trying to keep up with the 'stranger in the grey suit'. He took a taxi and managed to shake off his pursuers, either because the detectives couldn't get one themselves, or because they lost sight of him.

Luckily, they had made a note of the car's number plate and managed to track it down at its cab stand. The driver pointed them towards the Klomser. So off they went to the hotel. And here Redl alias Nizetas allegedly made two fundamental mistakes. First, he is said to have dropped scraps of paper that were later identified as receipts for two letters and a money transfer to a lieutenant in Stockerau. Secondly, he is said to have accidentally left his knife sheath in the taxi. According to the most popular version, it was left as 'lost property' at reception, where Redl recognised it when he was just about to leave the hotel.

Both incidents still seem inconceivable for an agent of his calibre, and given the lack of 100 per cent proven information nobody can fault us for suggesting that this was fabricated, yet another cover-up to hide someone's failure. In any case, Redl knew he was doomed. He probably even recognised the detectives that were positioned in and around the hotel. And the police officers recognised Redl, though none of them dared to arrest him, quite understandably.

They informed State Councillor and Head of Police Edmund von Gayer, who immediately got in touch with Ronge. He found the truth hard to believe. Redl had been his admired superior in the Evidenzbureau. Next in line was Urbański, who was even more disbelieving and is said to have rushed to the post office to compare handwriting. When he recognised his former deputy's fine writing, he lost every doubt. He was deeply shocked. But he had to act. Around 10pm he and Ronge interrupted the Chief of Staff's dinner at the Grand Hotel. It seems to have been Urbański who suggested allowing the disgraced officer to take his own life. Hoetzendorf agreed.

They decided to set up a delegation to pay the Colonel a visit. This took time. Many critics disapproved of the fact that Redl had been allowed to freely roam the city all evening. While the army officials tried to get a hold of their chosen candidates, Redl seems to have had a last encounter with his lover, Stefan Horinka, in his hotel room. We do not know what was said between them, but some of it we can imagine. If the newspaper articles that later told the story of a distressed Horinka who went to see Alfred's brother Heinrich and accused himself of being responsible for his suicide bear any truth, we may assume all had not ended well for the two, and that Horinka had carried out his threat and ended the relationship.

At around 8pm Generaladvokat Viktor Pollak came to pick Redl up for dinner in the restaurant Riedhof, followed by a visit to the coffeehouse Kaiserhof, another strange story that comes in a variety of versions. According to Pollak, the Colonel confided in him during dinner, without going into details. He asked for a gun which Pollak refused to get. He then begged him to arrange a safe passage to Prague for himself through the state police. Pollak did call Gayer at around 10pm and, according to the official statement given by the Defence Minister, he suggested having Redl institutionalised as he was convinced his friend had lost his mind.

This latter depiction fitted only too well with the army's initial attempts to declare Redl insane. Journalists also questioned other aspects of the story. Why had he asked for help from the state police? How come he hadn't told his old friend why precisely he intended to commit suicide? Maybe he was an accomplice, a lover? Had he been instructed to suggest suicide? Urbański claimed in his memoirs that none other than Archduke Franz Ferdinand himself had censored the Evidenzbureau's initial response to the parliamentarian interpellations.[2]

Gayer was said to have instructed Pollak to try and calm Redl down, and ask him to return to his hotel. Redl had allegedly anxiously waited for his friend's return from the public telephone, and looked horrified when Pollak whispered the results of his conversation in his ear. Whatever had been going on between them, Redl did return to his hotel. And around 12.30am on 25 May 1913 the army delegation finally turned up. It consisted of Urbański, Ronge, Auditor Vorliček and the Deputy Chief of the General Staff, Franz von Hoefer. Urbański remembered how he knocked on the door. Redl opened it and announced: 'I know why the gentlemen are here. I am the victim of a disastrous passion and would like to ask for a weapon to put an end to my existence.'[3] According to Georgi's statement in front of parliament Redl merely said: 'I know why the gentlemen are here, I feel guilty.'[4]

They all agreed later though that he had not tried to deny anything. He looked like a broken man. According to Hoefer, he asked the grace to die by his own hand. We have seen earlier that the Defence Minister mentioned a cord that had been lying on his bed, and a dagger on his desk, but not the Browning, which made the *Arbeiterzeitung* remark: 'So Redl shot himself with a dagger, or with a cord? It wouldn't have surprised anybody had Georgi suggested that as well.'[5]

He had already written two farewell letters, first to his Corps Commander, the second to one of his brothers. The delegation granted him his wish to write a third letter, a fact that was kept quiet.[6] According to Max Ronge Redl asked to confess to him alone. The three other men left the room. The Colonel begged Ronge to get him a gun. This he did, from the nearby War Ministry. Allegedly, he also picked up a deadly tapeworm remedy for his former superior, just in case.

Then Redl started his confession. According to Ronge's 1930

narrative he had provided foreign countries with the full range of materials in the course of 1910 and 1911. During his time in Prague he'd had to stick to a limited range. He delivered photographic reproductions, and worked without accomplices, knowing from experience that they usually meant the beginning of the end for the best of spies.

Contrary to this account, it is unlikely that Redl mentioned any other powers apart from Russia as his purchaser at this stage. Hoefer's notes for the Archduke contained no mention of Italy and France. These two countries seemed to have entered the scene only when Urbański examined the flat in Prague. And then there's the question why Redl only admitted to espionage in 'most recent times'. Was he ashamed to tell the full truth?

And what about Ronge's statements? We have mentioned the inconsistencies with details provided by the other delegates. As these were published seventeen years later, maybe his memory played tricks on him? But there is also a ludicrously short verbatim account he was asked to write down for the Archduke in June of the same year. Was it a reaction to all the criticism the delegates had to endure because of what was perceived by a majority of observers as a missed opportunity to get a full confession from a top spy, by allowing him to commit suicide?

Leidinger and Moritz reckon 'it seems as if everybody involved in the 'mission' (...) still saw the honourable friend in him. That he might have lied didn't occur to them at all, or only later on.' But maybe Ronge, who should later describe these 'hours, days and weeks as the saddest time of his life',[7] comparable only to the collapse of the Dual Monarchy in 1918 (strong words for man who lived through the loss of his own child), decided never to tell the full truth of what had been confessed to him that night. What if he had given his word of honour? He would have felt bound by it for the remainder of his days. Before the delegates left his room, Redl gave them the keys to his flat in Prague. The evidence they needed would all be in there.

The four delegates took position outside the hotel. They wore civilian clothing, trying not to cause a stir. But then they waited. And waited, for hours, and became nervous at sunrise when people started to take notice of the strange gathering in the street. Urbański suggested instructing a hotel porter to deliver an urgent letter to Redl. When he knocked on the Colonel's door and did not get a reply, he forced entry – and found him lying dead in his room.

Alfred Redl had shot himself in the mouth, at around 2am.

The initial post-mortem had been carried out quickly, and to be on the safe side Urbański ordered a thorough autopsy. The results that came in were only too handy for those who tried to excuse Redl's failures (and their own) with mental confusion. The pathologists found serious abnormal changes, especially chronic thickening of the soft and hard meninges, symptoms that point to the tertiary stage of syphilis. We know that Redl had caught syphilis years earlier, in 1891, while he attended military school. He was off sick for almost a year, until he was free of symptoms. But in those days there was no cure for syphilis.

The main substance used for treatment was mercury. Gerhard van Swieten, an Austrian army surgeon, had introduced the internal use of corrosive sublimate, mercuric chloride, in the eighteenth century. Guido Bacelli developed it as an injection in 1894. In the late nineteenth century, mercurous chloride (calomel), a purgative and laxative, was used as an unction, in tablet form and as an injection, and mercury ointments were developed. Mercury could have serious side effects such neuropathies, kidney failure, severe mouth ulcers, loss of teeth and deadly poisoning. Although more people died of its side effects than of the actual disease, it stayed in favour as treatment for syphilis until 1910 when Paul Ehrlich and Alfred Bertheim developed Salvarsan, also known as the 'magic bullet'.

The new treatment came years too late for Alfred Redl. Syphilis likes to show itself in different stages. After the initial infection with mild symptoms, it can remain latent for up to over thirty years. Around one-third of people develop tertiary syphilis. In around half of these patients showing tertiary-stage symptoms, the disease is physically disabling or fatal.

Of course it can't be ruled out that the pathologists made common cause with the military and fabricated the whole report. But even then, we still have Stefan Horinka's farewell letter:

> I would have taken your illness into account and had mercy, but I object to being forced or humiliated, I'm too proud for that. I won't agree to any such deal, I actually value my good health. What I did and what I intended to do was down to my friendship and understanding for you, you unfortunate (ill fated) man, but you can't force me.[8]

What Horinka might not have known at this point is that he actually carried the disease himself. This was diagnosed in the run-up to his trial. And although it is possible to transmit syphilis via non-sexual contact, it is very rare. Still, there was no sign of actual sexual penetration, and no proof that Redl had been the cause of his condition.

To us it seems that they both knew quite well what was happening. Redl knew that his days were numbered. He was old, he was ill. He was anxious not to lose his young lover. Horinka knew how desperate he was. It was not the first time he had threatened to leave Redl. In 1911 the 'uncle' had offered him the respectable amount of 100,000 kronen in exchange for his services. They settled on a different deal – the generous allowance with 'add-ons' for 'one monthly get-together for the purpose as defined by Colonel Redl'.[9]

On that last day of his life, our tragic antihero risked everything for the chance to change his lover's mind. He managed to retrieve the money deposited at the post office, he instantly transferred it to Stockerau. But he was no longer his old self. He knew he was being followed. He was emotionally drained and possibly mentally affected by his illness. If he really left his knife sheath in a taxi and fed his pursuers with scraps of paper that showed his handwriting as well as the recipient of his money transfer, look no further for an explanation. A top spy like Redl could not possibly make two fundamental mistakes like these in a row. Maybe this was his own way of admitting that he knew that his time had come.

Chapter 10

Legacy

The Redl Affair had everything: sex, espionage, betrayal, a fall from greatness and a sensational climax in which Redl went to his death like a figure of high tragedy.
(*New York Times*)

The old Emperor's response to the news about Redl's suicide seems to have been deep shock, anger and frustration. He had known the Colonel personally. According to press reports the messenger, Adjutant General Artur Freiherr von Bolfras, almost collapsed after he had witnessed Franz Joseph's reaction and exclaimed: 'I have never before seen His Majesty like this!'[1] Allegedly, the Emperor cried out in despair: 'So this is the new era, and the creatures it bears!'[2] Perhaps this was Redl's most telling obituary. His demise preceded the destruction of the old order by only a year. Perhaps the aged lion had an intimation of the cold bitter wind that would be blowing through his empty palaces. He'd have counted himself lucky he didn't live to see any of it.

Franz Ferdinand's reaction was much worse. He was well known for his screaming tantrums. Now he was absolutely furious. The military had failed left, right and centre. The whole situation was horribly embarrassing, criticism resounding from all ends of the Empire. Redl was said to have been his protégé, and Franz Ferdinand felt personally attacked. And there was something else the Archduke could not come to terms with. While his Emperor had approved of the decision to allow the doomed man to end his own life and save the face of the 'glorious army', this was incompatible with the faith of the ultra-Catholic heir.

He needed a fall-guy to vent his spleen on. He briefly condemned Conrad von Hoetzendorf – the earlier honeymoon period was very definitely over – then moved on to Urbański. When he accused him of sloppiness in his and Giesl's investigations in Prague, the Head of the Evidenzbureau tried to excuse his mistakes on the basis that his mental and physical health had been affected by the difficult circumstances. The Archduke lashed out at him. Quite obviously, he was no longer fit enough to do his job. His head was only spared thanks to support from the Chief of the General Staff himself, who found the best possible solution by granting his friend long-term personal leave.

Franz Ferdinand's fury against his target did not abate. Apparently, he even threatened to kill him should he come into his sight.[3] Throughout his life Urbański felt humiliated and treated unfairly. His rehabilitation was only feasible after the assassination.

Foreigners, especially diplomats, also felt the backlash from the affair. As was to be expected, Russians especially and in general were soon treated with suspicion. But other world powers did not escape either. In June 1913, the crisis touched the British Consulate in Sarajevo.[4] Two of its staff, Ernest MacFarren and John Hope-Johnstone, were interviewed (though not arrested) by the police. It turned out one had kept a notebook containing entries about k.u.k troops in the area, as well as other possibly suspicious information. MacFarren claimed he had only written down what was there for everyone to see anyway. Hope-Johnstone introduced himself as a linguist who had established contacts to Serbian citizens and Albanian refugees for the sole purpose of his research on 'Gipsy dialects'. An English bobby might have described both as 'likely stories'.

Needless to say, the Foreign Office was none too happy. It gave strict instructions to the British Consul in Sarajevo, F G Freeman, to avoid any further actions that could cause a stir. Foreign Minister Edward Grey even pondered Freeman's dismissal and the closure of the Consulate. The whole affair was especially embarrassing as MacFarren was also correspondent for the *Daily Mail*. The Austrian–

Hungarian external office made it perfectly clear to Military Attaché Cuninghame that they would welcome a change 'at the top of His Majesty's Consulate in Sarajevo'.

In the same month Cuninghame himself came under criticism when Captain Forbes, the British Consul in Prague, found out that his colleague had quizzed his own employees, primarily those of Austrian–Hungarian descent, about the movement of Habsburg's forces. Cuninghame gave a statement in which he denied any hostile motives. To improve bruised relations, he suggested permitting a higher number of k.u.k. officers to attend British manoeuvres, and ask for the same in return. This would make it easier to amass intelligence overtly. Both the War and Foreign Office approved of his idea.

Alfred Redl's failures became for many a means to an end. For the political left he was the personification of everything that was ailing in the Empire, and especially among its elite. Why should they be allowed their own legal system that enabled them to avoid civil jurisdiction? Why should everybody have to bow to them in awe? Occasionally their criticism combined with that of many officers who were opposed to any system of constant mutual spying that contrasted so starkly with notions of chivalry.

The conservatives, including the church, saw him as the victim of a rotten liberal ideology. *Danzers Armeezeitung* stated that the monarchy had experienced a 'moral *Koeniggraetz*' and claimed: 'We know officers who have refused to leave the house in other than civil clothing, and we know officers who are thinking about quitting. It is an unbearable thought to have been the comrade of a Redl.'[5]

The fact that Alfred Redl had been a high-ranking officer fuelled an ongoing debate that had originated in the eighteenth century. Should non-aristocrats be allowed to become officers at all? Back then the majority of gentry had regarded soldiering predominantly as a means of self-enrichment. The system had become corrupt and inefficient, and its overhaul was part of Empress Maria Theresa's deep cutting reforms.[6]

She created a military system funded through taxation, commanded by professionals and with restricted opportunities for financial gain. She had initially hoped to be able to recruit her senior officers from the high ranks of the nobility. Not only did the state lack the necessary cash to finance their remuneration but the hereditary military elite were not enthusiastic about fighting for wages. Feudal service was traditionally unwaged but the lord would expect to be well rewarded from the spoils of victory. A regular salary cheque lacked the same allure.

A rather more pressing issue presented itself in the realisation these people were 'amateurs' and not necessarily interested in equipping themselves with the complicated specialist knowledge required to fight industrial wars. During Bismarck's wars, artillery tripled in numbers and field engineering became infinitely more complex. The noble families remained reluctant to send their offspring to the newly formed *Militaerakademien*. Over time, this led to the acceptance of pupils from all classes of society to the academies. War was becoming a science for professionals rather than a sport for gentlemen.

In the High Middle Ages, the redoubtable mercenary knight Götz von Berlichingen, poet, swashbuckler and swordsman typified the gentleman warrior. He sold his sword to whoever was paying and lost a hand to the diabolical new science of gunnery. Undeterred, he acquired a workable prosthetic and carried on much as before in a career that spanned nearly half a century – legendary as 'Götz of the Iron Hand'.[7]

Götz and Alfred wouldn't have had much to talk about, even though both were motivated by cash. Working as a gentleman mercenary was an acceptable profession in the fifteenth century but being a commoner spy in the twentieth was not. The Austrian elite belonged to that chivalric tradition (pretty rough and ready in its own way). Their ideals harked back to this golden age of knighthood. Redl represented the cold wind of a new set of realities. No more glorious charges like Sobieski's winged hussars sweeping down like the wrath of God upon the infidel and delivering Vienna. War was about technologies, supply and logistics, campaigns decided only by attrition. Gettysburg should have ended the American Civil War – it didn't. There was a clear lesson there but nobody was really looking.

Redl represented the new face of war and espionage. Spying has always been part of the game but industrial wars merit industrial spying. Redl was a professional – disloyal, duplicitous and amoral but still a pro. Franz Joseph might shudder, Franz Ferdinand might rage, but this was the new reality. His way of life would outlast theirs.

Those who'd lost privileges in the process together with core reactionaries had still not fully accepted these changes. With Redl they saw a trump card. He was the evidence that 'commoners' could only bring ruin to the military. And they found their most prominent advocate in the Archduke, who now started to demand a higher percentage of aristocrats in the officer corps. Nobody could call Franz Ferdinand an innovator.

The *Arbeiterzeitung* reminded their opponents that even the noblest descent did not protect against serious deceit, the most prominent and dire example being General Baron von Eynatten. He'd been made responsible for feeding the army but really cared only for his own profits and let his men starve. The Baron's defalcation became a major factor in losing the Lombardy campaign. The paper also pointed to the initial reasons for opening up the higher military career to all social classes: 'The Austrian army would still be as aristocratic as it used to be, had the owners of those most noble names not decided to run away from the requirements the service demanded.'[9]

Numerous journalists brought the Empire's ethnic conflicts into sharp focus. All of a sudden Redl had Polish blood. To the Hungarians it was clear that his background was Ruthenian. Then at last, and perhaps inevitably, Redl became a Jew, despite his Catholic background. It was claimed that his mother's maiden name was Sternberg. Others modified this statement by asserting she was born in a place of the same name, so they declared him a 'third generation Jew'. This wasn't the end of it. The old spy continued to get dragged out of his coffin wherever an ideology needed a bogeyman. The Nazis would revive the myth of his Jewish background in 1938 and claim that Alfred changed his surname from 'Redlich' (also German for 'honest', 'upright') to 'Redl'.

Had the Austrian Empire outlasted the war it had begun, Redl might have earned more widespread fame or notoriety but the whole system collapsed in 1918 and the old order just became old. The map of the world had changed dramatically. Of the great empires, Russia, Germany, Austria and Turkey were destroyed. Britain and France survived but scarred, ruined and depleted. French morale had not recovered by 1940. Some scholars like John Keegan became convinced Britain never fully recovered from the Somme.

Some of the old Buchan-esque ideas about spying as an affair for gentlemen lingered. Heydrich modelled the SD on the British Secret Service on the basis that they were both successful and 'gentlemen' – a caste he yearned to belong to. This lingered. It wasn't until the debacle of the Cambridge Spies blew up in the faces of MI6 that a cold new reality dawned. John Le Carré who knows a thing or two about spies recalled a conversation with Philby's former close friend and colleague Nicholas Elliott, over twenty years after the scandal:

> But the limited truth, the digestible version: namely, in Elliott's jargon, that somewhere back in the war years when it was understandable, Kim had gone a bit squidgy about our gallant Russian ally and given him a bit of this and that; and if he could just get it off his chest, whatever it was he'd given them, we'd all feel a lot better, and he could get on with doing what he did best, which was beating the Russian at his own game.[10]

Nobody was ever going to call Alfred Redl 'squidgy'. But then he was never an insider like Philby, never really one of 'us'. He was a pleb, an oik up from the provinces; useful, clever, even necessary, but still not quite a gentleman.

The case remained a hot topic over the next two decades. It is not difficult to understand that the story with its explosive personal, social and political dimensions was and still is irresistible to a wide spectrum of creative artists; the fascination of the tragic and unexplained has kept several generations of them busy. The lack of any final, proven truth, the legions of rumours, half-truths and lies made it easy for them to invent their own fictional variants. And the same writers and filmmakers who kept the spy's memory alive often found themselves under fire from all sides.

Egon Erwin Kisch, whose representations of the case have managed to dominate general awareness until today, still drew hostility even in the 1960s and got disparaged for being a 'Jew and a Socialist'.[11] 'Harmless' movies such as *Oberst Redl* (1925), or *Der Fall des Generalstabs – Oberst Redl* (1931) were closely scrutinised and received a continuous stream of criticism from military circles who objected to seeing the former Emperor and the dynasty dragged through the dirt.

When Franz Antel announced a new film project in the 1950s, monarchists, amongst them former k.u.k. officers of venerable age, launched a storm of protest.[12] This came as a bit of a surprise. The filmmaker, who has produced a number of glorious films during his long career which have become classics both on Austrian and German screens, had previously received plenty of praise from the same crowd, for productions such as the *Emperor Waltz* and the *Emperor's Ball*. Now they saw Austria's dignity and reputation under threat and tried to embargo the whole production. They even managed to find an ally in the Education Ministry who voted against the film's export to Germany (which would have spelt its financial ruin), for 'moral and patriotic' reasons, especially as he believed the film 'hinted at Redl's unfortunate disposition'.

After assuring themselves that *Spionage* would not feature 'anti-Austrian' sentiments the authorities gave Antel the green light. The film has recently (2015) become available again on DVD. It is principally enjoyable because of an excellent cast. For an 'espionage thriller' it lacks excitement; historically, it mainly follows Kisch's fictional account with an added femme fatale. The 'mysterious woman' became an integral part of novels and films alike. This is hardly surprising, not least because Redl's homosexuality remained an area most artists did not dare to touch.

When John Osborne broke the unwritten rule and made the Colonel's homosexuality the subject of his play *A Patriot for Me* in 1965, it was not officially allowed on stage at the Royal Court Theatre. Apparently it was 'too sexually transgressive' (whatever that means). The only way it could be shown at all was to declare the theatre a 'private club' for the duration of the performances.[13]

Amongst the countless takes on the subject amongst writers, Robert Asprey's semi-fictional *A Panther's Feast* (1959) is one we need to mention, not just because unlike most others it is available in English. Asprey, himself an ex-US intelligence officer based in Austria after 1945, became obsessed with the case and started his own research. He delved into archives as well as interviewing witnesses, whose trustworthiness might have been compromised by the fact that they got paid for delivering information. From a historian's perspective it is rather disappointing that he turned his research into a quasi-novel of questionable qualities.

The 1980s brought a new perspective with Péter Dobai's novel *Roman ueber die Donaumonarchie*. His Redl was also a corrupt character, but one who had become the victim of a dysfunctional society. Dobai co-wrote the screenplay for Istvan Szabó's award-winning film *Colonel Redl* from 1985, with the charismatic Klaus Maria Brandauer in the title role and Armin Mueller-Stahl as the Archduke. Again, Redl's homosexuality is only hinted at, although his longings and inner conflicts are illustrated beautifully. He is a sympathetic character, an outsider who doesn't fit in anywhere.

When one 'googles' the name Alfred Redl these days, the old stereotypes still dominate search results. We find the reckless spy, the 'homosexual who wrecked an empire'. Hopefully this book will manage to further de-demonise our man and show him as what he was: not your ordinary human being, not innocent, but not evil either.

For quite a while after Redl's death in 1913 the Evidenzbureau kept his alter ego Nizetas alive, hoping to catch another spy or two.

Redl was never allowed to rest in peace. 'Patriots' started to vandalise his grave in June the same year. In 1944 his mortal remains were moved further down as the space was needed for a new arrival.

This hasn't prevented him from staying on the loose since. Regardless of how many jigsaw pieces we manage to add to the picture, ultimately his persona will remain a mystery. Alfred Redl's compelling story is far from dead. In some ways he is a metaphor for the modern world, ambitious but without a place, craving recognition in a system from which he is effectively disbarred.

Notes

Chapter 1

1. Stefan Zweig, *The World of Yesterday* (1943), p. 25.
2. Egon Erwin Kisch, *Das tätowierte Porträt* (1976), p. 457.
3. Jan Richter, *Egon Erwin Kisch – the Raging Reporter*, Prague Radio 27 September 2011.
4. *Die Zeit*, 27 May 1913, p. 5.
5. Egon Erwin Kisch, *Sensation Fair: Tales of Prague*, Kindle edn, loc. 5874.
6. Ibid., loc. 5510 et seq.
7. Otto Friedlaender, *Letzter Glanz der Maerchenstadt* (1948), p. 336.
8. *Die Arbeiterzeitung*, 29 May 1913, pp. 6–7.
9. *Die Arbeiterzeitung*, 31 May 1913, pp. 1–4.
10. *Das Fremdenblatt*, 30 May 1913, pp. 9–10.
11. Kisch, *Sensation Fair*, loc. 5614 et seq.
12. *Die Arbeiterzeitung*, 31 May 1913, p. 4.
13 *Die Arbeiterzeitung*, 6 June 1913, pp. 5–7.

Chapter 2

1. First published in 1940 by RCS Media Group.
2. Directed by Valerio Zurlini, released in the UK in January 1978.
3. In Polish Lvov and in Latin, Leopolis.
4. A voivodeship is a region administered by a viodode or governor.
5. R Asprey, *The Panther's Feast* (1959), p. 21.
6. The gulden, divided into 60 kreuzer, was the standard unit of currency between 1754 and 1892, when replaced by the krone which followed the gold standard, roughly equal to £6.00–£7.00 in today's money.
7. Jozef Klemens Pilsudski (1867–1935), perhaps the father of Polish independence and winner of the decisive Battle of Warsaw 1920.

8. Wlaydyslaw Sikorski (1881–1943), Polish leader during the Nazi occupation, his death in a plane crash remains suspicious.

9. Kazimierz Sosnkowski (1885–1969), aristocrat, diplomat and freedom fighter.

10. Moritz von Auffenburg-Komarow, *Aus Osterreichs Hoehe und Niedergang*, quoted in Asprey, *Panther's Feast*, pp. 24–5.

11. Asprey, *Panther's Feast*, p. 25.

12. https://en.wikipedia.org/wiki/Volksschule, retrieved October 2015.

13. Royal Military Academy, Sandhurst, *War Studies: A Textbook for the 21st Century British Officer* (version 4.1, July 2004), p. 27.

14. The death toll in the earlier conflict is put at 8 million, twice that of the Napoleonic Wars, ibid.

15. Ibid.

16. Ibid., p. 33.

17. Ibid., p. 35.

18. P Hennessey, *The Junior Officers Reading Club* (2009), p. 54.

19. Asprey, *Panther's Feast*, p. 29.

20. Ibid., p. 173.

21. Ibid., p. 171.

22. Quoted ibid..

23. The Ottomans divided territories into districts and sub-districts or sanjaks – the Sanjak of Novibazar was part of the wider region of Kosovo and thus at the very heart of the old kingdom of Serbia.

24. E Crankshaw, *The Fall of the House of Habsburg* (1963), p. 330.

25. The Young Turks had ousted the last Sultan in 1908 and ushered in an era of limited democratic rule under a constitutional monarchy.

26. Ibid., p. 329.

27. Ibid., p. 330.

28. The 'Pig Wars' was an attempt or series of attempts by the Empire to exert economic coercion against Serbia by banning the import of pigs, the country's most important export, ibid., p. 333.

29. Ibid., p. 336.

30. *Pascali's Island* was published by Michael Joseph in 1980. The film starring Ben Kingsley, Charles Dance and Helen Mirren, directed by James Dearden, was released in May 1988.

Chapter 3

1. L B Namier, 'The Downfall of the Habsburg Monarchy', in *Vanished Supremacies* (1962), p. 139.

2. A nineteenth-century movement aiming for unity of all the Slavic peoples.

3. P Jung, *The Austrian Forces in World War 1 (1) 1914–1916* (2003), p. 5.

4. Ibid., p. 3.

5. Ibid., p. 4.

6. J Keegan, *The First World War* (Pimlico 1999), pp. 219–220.

7. Jung, *Austrian Forces*, p. 34.

8. Recounted in Asprey, *Panther's Feast*, p. 39.

9. Jung, *Austrian Forces*, p. 35.

10. That rich belt of Northern Italy, with capitals at Milan and Venice.

11. J W Mason, *The Dissolution of the Austro-Hungarian Empire 1867–1918* (2013), p. 4, and Crankshaw, *House of Habsburg*, pp. 13–14.

12. From a long established noble family and the Emperor's brother in law, Crankshaw, *House of Habsburg*, p. 44.

13. Baron Alexander von Bach (1813–93)

14. The Swiss Jean-Henri Dunant, though he did not witness the fighting, toured the field in the immediate aftermath – an experience which triggered the founding of the Red Cross and the basis for the Geneva Convention.

15. Mason, *Dissolution*, p. 7, and Crankshaw, *House of Habsburg*, pp. 238–40.

16. Mason, *Dissolution*, p. 7, and Crankshaw, *House of Habsburg*, pp. 238–40.

17. Mason, *Dissolution*, p. 9, and Crankshaw, *House of Habsburg*, p. 240.

18. Primarily an area now covered by the Ukraine.

19. A region north of Croatia, centred on Ljubljana.

20. Mason, *Dissolution*, p. 14, and A J P Taylor, *The Hapsburg Monarchy* (1972 edn), pp. 91, 93.

21. Mason, *Dissolution*, pp. 14–15, and Taylor, *Hapsburg Monarchy*,

pp. 91, 93.

22. Mason, *Dissolution*, p. 21, and Crankshaw, *House of Habsburg*, p. 243.

23. Quoted, in Mason, *Dissolution*, p. 22, and Crankshaw, *House of Habsburg*, p. 275.

24. Mason, *Dissolution*, p. 24, and Crankshaw, *House of Habsburg*, p. 275.

25. Countess Zanardi Landi, *Is Austria Doomed* (1916), p. 53.

26. Mason, *Dissolution*, p. 32.

27. Ibid., p. 33, and Crankshaw, *House of Habsburg*, p. 187.

28. Mason, *Dissolution*, p. 35, and Crankshaw, *House of Habsburg*, p. 273.

29. Mason, *Dissolution*, p. 40.

30. Ibid. and Crankshaw, *House of Habsburg*, pp. 300–2.

31. Mason, *Dissolution*, p. 41, and Crankshaw, *House of Habsburg*, pp. 275, 294.

32. Quoted in Mason, *Dissolution*, p. 42.

33. Ibid.

Chapter 4

1. Directed by Terence Young and released in October 1962.

2. Made for ITV, directed by Martin Campbell and Jim Goddard, first aired in September 1983.

3. Sidney Reilly (1874–1925), perhaps truly the 'Ace of Spies' and possible model for Bond.

4. J Keegan, *Intelligence in War* (2003), p. 1.

5. Ibid., pp. 3–4.

6. G Milton, *Russian Roulette* (2013), pp. 54–6.

7. Ibid., pp. 58–9.

8. http://gizmodo.com/13-of-historys-most-ingenious-spy-cameras-1685088759, retrieved October 2015.

9. D Stevenson, *Armaments and the Coming of War 1909–1914* (1996), p. 49.

10. Ibid.

11. Ibid.

12. Ibid., p. 50.

13. Ibid.

14. Ibid.

15. Ibid.

16. Published by Arrow in 2014.

17. M Cornwall, 'Traitors and the Meaning of Treason in Austro-Hungary's Great War', *Transactions of the Royal Historical Society*, 25 (2015), p. 126.

18. Ibid., p 116.

19. Ibid.

20. Ibid.

21. Ibid., p. 119.

22. Ibid., pp. 121–2.

23. Ibid., p. 120.

24. Ibid., p. 121.

25. L Cole, *Military Culture and Popular Patriotism in Late Imperial Austria* (2014), p. 308.

26. Ibid., pp. 308–9.

27. Ibid., p. 309.

28. Ibid.

Chapter 5

1. Cornwall, 'Traitors', p. 115.

2. Ibid., p. 117.

3. Ibid., p. 119.

4. Ibid., p. 123.

5. Ibid., p. 124.

6. http://www.tourmycountry.com/austria/kriegsministerium.htm, retrieved October 2015.

7. Ibid.

8. Wladimir Rudolf Karl Freiherr Giesl von Gieslingen (1860–1936).

9. The following descriptions of court cases are based on Asprey's narrative.

10. http://uk.businessinsider.com/interview-barry-royden-former-

director-of-counterintelligence-for-the-cia-2015-5?r=US&IR=T, retrieved November 2015.

Chapter 6

1. The main findings in this chapter are based on Leidinger and Moritz, *Oberst Redl* (2012) and Gerhard Jagschitz et al., *Im Zentrum der Macht* (2007).
2. Asprey, *Panther's Feast*, p. 123.
3. Conrad von Hoetzendorf, *Aus meiner Dienstzeit, 1906–1918* (1921), vol. 3, p. 345.
4. *Arbeiterzeitung*, 5 June 1913, p. 7.
5. Asprey, *Panther's Feast*, p. 179.
6. It is impossible to translate the word *razvedka* precisely into any foreign language. It is usually translated as 'reconnaissance' or 'spying' or 'intelligence gathering'. A fuller explanation of the word is that it describes any means and any actions aimed at obtaining information about an enemy, analysing it and understanding it properly.
7. Ronge, *Kriegs-und Industriespionage: Zwölf Jahre Kundschaftsdienst* (1930), p. 25.
8. Leidinger and Moritz, *Oberst Redl*, loc. 2207.
9. *Arbeiterzeitung*, 30 May 1913, p. 1.
10. See Federal Chancellery Austria, *Vienna Modernism 1890–1910* (1999).
11. Karl Kraus, *Aphorismen: Länder und Leute* (East Berlin, 1971), ch. 8.
12. See, for example, Arthur Schnitzler, *Therese, Chronik eines Frauenlebens* (The Chronicle of a Woman's Life) (Berlin, 1928).
13. *Arbeiterzeitung*, 18 June 1913, pp. 7–8.

Chapter 7

1. G Bischof et al., *1914* (2014), p. xiii.
2. Sophie Duchess of Hohenburg (1868–1914), though of Bohemian aristocratic blood, wasn't eligible to become empress consort so the marriage was strictly morganatic.
3. The car still survives.

4. Princip stated he'd not intended to shoot Sophie; he was aiming for the governor.

5. Jung, *Austrian Forces*, p. 9.

6. Ibid.

7. Ibid., p. 10.

8. Ibid., p. 11.

9. H Leidinger, 'The Case of Alfred Redl and the Situation of Austro-Hungarian Military Intelligence on the Eve of World War I', in Bischof et al., *1914*, p. 35.

10. Ibid.

11. Ibid., pp. 36–7.

12. Ibid.

13. Ibid., p. 37.

14. Ibid.

15. According to Leidinger and Moritz, *Oberst Redl*, loc. 2966, some of these materials were actually sold, but no further evidence is given.

16. Leidinger, 'Case of Alfred Redl', p. 39.

17. Ibid.

18. Ibid.

19.. Ibid.

20 Ibid., p. 40.

21. Ibid., p. 41.

22. Ibid.

23. Ibid., p. 42.

24. Ibid., p. 44.

25. Ibid.

26. Ibid., p. 45.

27. Ibid.

28. Ibid., p. 46.

29. Ibid.

30. Ibid.

31. Ibid.

32. Ibid. p. 48.

33. The Balkan crisis comprised two wars, 1912 and 1913, the first

when the Balkan states fought Turkey and the second when they fought amongst themselves. Serbia was the chief winner.

34. Ibid., p. 49.
35. Ibid.
36. Ibid., p. 50.
37. Ibid., p. 51.
38. Ibid.
39. Ibid.

Chapter 8

1. *Fremdenblatt*, 1 June 1913, p. 11.
2. *Herald Tribune*, 31 March 1951.
3. Leidinger and Moritz, *Oberst Redl*, loc. 2657.
4. Ibid., loc. 2692.
5. Geoffrey W Bateman, 'Austria', *The glbtq Encyclopedia*.
6. Sarah Lavender, 'A Legacy Restored: A Study of Oscar Wilde's Public Perception over Time', SIRP-NCHC Conference 2011, p. 4.
7. *Maehrisches Tagblatt*, 28 November 1902, p. 1.
8. See John C G Röhl, *The Kaiser and his Court* (1987).
9. *Danzer Armeezeitung*, 5 June 1913, p. 1.

Chapter 9

1. Both Max Ronge and August Urbański tell this version of the story, see Leidinger and Moritz, *Oberst Redl*, loc. 1336.
2. Conrad von Hoetzendorf, *Aus meiner Dienstzeit*, vol. 3, p. 345.
3. Leidinger and Moritz, *Oberst Redl*, loc. 1672 et seq.
4. *Arbeiterzeitung*, 6 June 1913, p. 1.
5. Ibid.
6. Sequence of events according to research by Leidinger and Moritz, *Oberst Redl*, loc. 1708 et seq.
7. Ronge, *Kriegs- und Industriespionage*, p. 76.
8. Leidinger and Moritz, *Oberst Redl*, loc. 2690.
9. Ibid., loc. 26.

Chapter 10

NOTES

1. *Arbeiterzeitung*, 2 June 1913, p. 3.
2. Freiherr von Margutti, ‚Vom alten Kaiser‘, in Leidinger and Moritz, *Oberst Redl*, loc. 1618.
3. Ibid., loc. 3098.
4. Ibid., loc. 3288 et seq.
5. *Danzers Armeezeitung*, 5 June 1913, p. 5.
6. See Gunther E Rothenberg, 'Nobility and Military Careers: The Habsburg Officer Corps, 1740–1914', *Military Affairs*, 40.4 (1 December 1976), p. 182 et seq.
7. Hugh Chisholm (ed.), 'Berlichingen, Goetz‘ in *Encyclopaedia* (11th edn, Cambridge, 1911), vol. 3.
8. *Die Arbeiterzeitung*, 4 June 1913, p. 7.
9. Leidinger and Moritz, *Oberst Redl*, loc. 4578.
10. B Macintyre, *A Spy Among Friends* (2014), p. 289.
11. Leidinger and Moritz, *Oberst Redl*, loc 4578.
12. *Der Spiegel*, 'O du mein Österreich', 23 February 1955, pp. 38–40.
13. Renate Wagner, Review *Oberst Redl – Ein Patriot*, Scala Theatre Vienna, 2015, http://der-neue-merker.eu/wien-scala-oberst-redl-ein-patriot.

Select Bibliography

Asprey, R, *The Panther's Feast* (New York, 1959)

Baedeker, *Austria-Hungary* (Leipzig, 1911)

Bateman, Geoffrey W, 'Austria', in *The glbtq Encyclopaedia*, http://www.glbtqarchive.com

Beer, Siegfried, 'Die Nachrichtendienste in der Habsburgermonarchie', *SIAK-Journal – Zeitschrift für Polizeiwissenschaft und polizeiliche Praxis*, 3 (1917): 53–63

Bill, Claus Heinrich, *Selbstentleibungen im deutschen vormodernen Adel* (Kiel, 2013), http://home.foni.net/~adelsforschung2/floriankuehnel.htm

Bischof, Günter, et al., *1914: Austria-Hungary, the Origins, and the First Year of World War I*, Contemporary Austrian Studies (New Orleans and Innsbruck, 2014)

Cole, L, *Military Culture and Popular Patriotism in Late Imperial Austria* (Oxford, 2014)

Cornwall, M, 'Traitors and the Meaning of Treason in Austro-Hungary's Great War', *Transactions of the Royal Historical Society*, 25 (Cambridge, 2015): 113–34

Crankshaw, E, *The Fall of the House of Hapsburg* (London, 1963)

Der Spiegel, 'O du mein Österreich', 23 February 1955, 38–40

Der Spiegel, 'Schwule wie die Brennesseln entfernen', 6 January 1984, 25–8

Federal Chancellery Austria, *Vienna Modernism, 1890–1910* (Vienna, 1999)

Friedlaender, Otto, *Der letzte Glanz der Marchenstadt: Letzter Glanz der Märchenstadt – Wien um 1900* (Vienna, 1948)

Greenberg, David F, *The Construction of Homosexuality* (Chicago, 1988)

Hennessey, P., *The Junior Officers Reading Club* (London, 2009)

Hoetzendorf, Conrad von, *Aus meiner Dienstzeit, 1906–1918*, vols

1–3 (Vienna, 1921)

Jagschitz, Gerhard, Leidinger, Hannes, and Moritz, Verena, *Im Zentrum der Macht: Die vielen Gesichter des Geheimdienstchefs Maximilian Ronge* (Vienna, 2007)

Jung, P, *The Austrian Forces in World War 1: 1. 1914–1916*, Osprey 'Men at Arms' series no. 392.

Keegan, J, *The First World War* (Pimlico, 1999)

Keegan, J, *Intelligence in War* (London, 2003)

Kisch, Egon Erwin, *Das Taetowierte Portrait* (Leipzig, 1976)

Kisch, Egon Erwin, *Sensation Fair: Tales of Prague* (Kindle Edition 2012)

Kronenbitter, Günther, *'Krieg im Frieden': Die Führung der k.u.k. Armee und die Großmachtpolitik österreich-Ungarns 1906–1914* (Munich, 2003)

Landi, Countess Zanardi, *Is Austria Doomed* (London, 1916)

Lavender, Sarah, 'A Legacy Restored: A Study of Oscar Wilde's Public Perception over Time', SIRP–NCHC Conference 2011

Leidinger, Hannes, Moritz Verena, *Oberst Redl: Der Spionagefall, der Skandal, die Fakten* (Kindle Edition 2012)

Leidinger, Hannes, 'The Case of Alfred Redl and the Situation of Austro-Hungarian Military Intelligence on the Eve of World War I', in Günter Bischof et al., *1914: Austria-Hungary, the Origins, and the First Year of World War I* (New Orleans and Innsbruck, 2014)

Macintyre, B, *A Spy among Friends* (London, 2014)

Márai, Sándor, *Embers* (New York, 2001)

Mason, J W, *The Dissolution of the Austro-Hungarian Empire 1867–1918* (Abingdon, 2013)

Milton, G, *Russian Roulette* (London, 2013)

Namier, L B, 'The Downfall of the Habsburg Monarchy', in *Vanished Supremacies* (Harmondsworth, 1962)

Ottosson, Cathrine, *über den Tod und die Ehre in der Novelle Leutnant Gustl von Arthur Schnitzler* (Stockholm, 2007)

Richter, Jan, *Egon Erwin Kisch – the Raging Reporter*, Radio Prague 27 September 2011

SELECT BIBLIOGRAPHY

Röhl, John C., *Philipp Eulenburgs politische Korrespondenz: Von der Reichsgründung bis zum Neuen Kurs, 1866–1891* (Munich, 1976)

Röhl, John C., *The Kaiser and his Court: Wilhelm II and the Government of Germany* (Cambridge, 1987)

Ronge, Max, *Kriegs-und Industriespionage: Zwölf Jahre Kundschaftsdienst* (Vienna and Leipzig, 1930)

Rothenberg, Gunther E, 'Nobility and Military Careers: The Habsburg Officer Corps, 1740–1914', *Military Affairs*, 40/4(1 December 1976): 182–6

Royal Military Academy, *War Studies: A Textbook for the 21st Century British Officer*, version 4.1 (Sandhurst, July 2004)

Smith, Duncan J, 'Vienna – beneath the Austrian Capital', *Hidden Europe* (27 July 2009), 22–7

Sombart, Nicolaus, *Wilhelm II. Sündenbock und Herr der Mitte* (Berlin, 1996)

Steakley, James D, 'Iconography of a Scandal', in *Hidden from History* (London, 1991)

Stevenson, D., *Armaments and the Coming of War 1909–1914* (Oxford, 1996)

Taylor A J P, *The Habsburg Monarchy* (London, 1972 edn)

Wheatcroft, A, *The Habsburgs* (London, 1995)

Zweig, Stefan, *The World of Yesterday: An Autobiography* (New York, 1943)

SELECT BIBLIOGRAPHY

Index

INDEX

Harden, Maximilian 129
Hardinge, Charles 39
Harrach, Colonel von 104, 105
Hekajlo, Sigmund 89
Hillebrand, Delegate 18
Hirschfeld, Magnus 128
Hitler, Adolf 21
Hochverrat 68
Hoefer, Franz von 136
Hoetzendorf, General Conrad
  von 13, 38, 45, 64, 89, 92, 93,
  106, 108, 113, 117, 118, 119,
  123, 142
Hope-Johnstone, John 142
Hordliczka, Colonel Eugen 83,
  85, 88
Horrowitz, Michael 6
Hotel Klomser 1, 11, 12, 13,
  134
Horinka, Stephan Lieutenant 12,
  15, 16, 123, 125, 126, 127,
  133, 139

I

Investigation of a Citizen above
  Suspicion 101
Istria 37
Izvolsky, Alexander 38, 39

J

Jandrić, Alexander 96, 108
Jandrić, Cedomil 96, 97, 108
Javurek, Gunner 47

K

Kaution 25
Keegan, Sir John 58
Kerensky's Provisional
  Government 61
Kienbusch, Alfred Kretschmar
  von 95
Kim 60
Kingdom of Ruthenia 24
Kipling 60
Kisch, Egon Irwin 2, 4, 5, 89,
  147
Koerber, von 54
Korner, Theodor 94
Kraft-Ebing, Richard 128
Kraus, Karl 99
Krupp, Friedrich Alfred 128, 129
Kucirek, Wenzel 6, 14

L

Landi, Countess 53
Langer Robert 109
Lawrow, Simon 83, 84
Le Carré, John 146
Leidinger, Hannes 98, 114, 119,
  134, 137
Lemberg 21, 24, 25, 26, 27, 34,
  77, 92, 118
Leuthner, Delegate von, 17, 18
Lincoln, President 60
Lojka, Leopold 105
Lombardy 37, 49
Louis XIV 70